To dear ...
much lo... ...fulness
for a delightful friendship!
Susan

A HOME ON HIGH

HUSBAND FATHER CHRISTIAN MUSICIAN POET TEACHER

Nick Miller
1953-2015

A HOME ON HIGH

HUSBAND FATHER CHRISTIAN MUSICIAN POET TEACHER

Nick Miller

1953-2015

MEREO

Cirencester

Mereo Books
1A The Wool Market Dyer Street Cirencester Gloucestershire GL7 2PR
An imprint of Memoirs Publishing www.mereobooks.com

A home on high: 978-1-86151-602-2

First published in Great Britain in 2016
by Mereo Books, an imprint of Memoirs Publishing

A CIP catalogue record for this book is available from the British Library.

The address for Memoirs Publishing Group Limited can be found at www.memoirspublishing.com

The Memoirs Publishing Group Ltd Reg. No. 7834348

The Memoirs Publishing Group supports both The Forest Stewardship Council® (FSC®) and the PEFC® leading international forest-certification organisations. Our books carrying both the FSC label and the PEFC® and are printed on FSC®-certified paper. FSC® is the only
forest-certification scheme supported by the leading environmental organisations including Greenpeace. Our paper procurement policy can be found at www.memoirspublishing.com/environment

Typeset in 10/15pt Century Schoolbook
by Wiltshire Associates Publisher Services Ltd. Printed and bound in Great Britain by Printondemand-Worldwide, Peterborough PE2 6XD

CONTENTS

INTRODUCTION AND THANKS

This precious account was dictated by Nick in the weeks before his last Christmas, 2014.

Thanks to several kind friends of the remarkable Jodie Casson for typing these memoirs, which, accompanied by tea and gentle conversation, characterised many shared afternoons.

Special thanks go to Heidi Maccanti for her unfailing support along the way. Sharing this journey was never going to be easy, and Heidi helped so much with her sunny attitude and encouragement.

We are indebted to the worldwide church family for the many varied expressions of compassionate love and care. New Creation Church Singapore, Union Church HK and The Vine Church HK, thank you for standing with us when we could not stand any longer.

To the schools we worked at, thank you for the opportunity. Nick was never happier than when enabling young people to walk strongly into all the promise that life can bring. It was an enormous privilege to work in these outstanding educational settings with joy and purpose.

And to all the musical companions, collaborators and co-creators over the years – thanks for being such a great band of brothers! Nick especially loved making, sharing and playing music with others and true community was enjoyed in this way. Praise to the One from whom all creativity flows.

Many dear family members, friends and colleagues visited Nick at home in his final days, none of us realising how short his time was actually going to be. Thank you to each one for adding your own special touch to this time.

Nick very much wanted to set down in print the enduring memories and influences which shaped his life, hoping they might be of some interest to family and friends. It was a source of joy to him to have so much to be thankful for and to see his final creative project realised.

And for those friends who have joined us round our table, yes these are the dinner party stories!

Alison Miller

Nick's final album, "Home", is available on iTunes.

CHAPTER ONE

ORIGINS

I was born in the 1950s, one of the Baby Boomers, part of the generation that was fortunate enough never to have been called to take up arms for my country; that generation whose parents were irrevocably scarred by war.

My father, Jim, had trained to be a bank manager at Barclays. He saw war on the horizon and joined the Territorial Army. He was right; the war would catch up with England. When it came, he was a soldier in the Royal Artillery. He was also quite a sensitive guy in his own way, with a passion for music. He learned to play the double bass from the bass player in Bert Ambrose's orchestra. Living in Wimbledon, he played in dance bands performing all around London. He used to say that he earned much more from his music gigs than from his banking job. His own father was an architect who had moved down from Morpeth, Northumberland, to follow his profession.

Jim's first assignment as a soldier was to join the first army in North Africa. He was on board a troop ship called the *Strathallan*, part of a large troop convoy accompanied by destroyers heading for North Africa to fight Rommel and his Africa Corps. In the middle of the night in the Mediterranean Sea, a torpedo fired by a German U boat struck his ship. The lights immediately went out and the ship began to sink, then caught fire.

He was fortunate enough to have a torch. Following a tussle with another soldier over his torch, he was able to lead the way out of the cabin and onto the deck, where he jumped into the sea. He told me of the horror of seeing wooden rafts being thrown from the deck of the sinking ship onto the heads of people who had escaped the burning *Strathallan*. He was one of the lucky ones. The destroyer escort, captained by 'Beaky' Armstrong, came alongside and my father was able to scramble up the netting to safety. The destroyer didn't hang around long in case it collected its own torpedo.

Forever afterwards Jim slept with a torch beside his bed. Armstrong's destroyer was itself eventually the victim of a German torpedo, fired by a U boat which they believed was surrendering. I remember as a teenager seeing Jim weeping on the anniversary of Armstrong's death.

Jim eventually joined up with the First Army, and found himself in command of a number of 25-pounder guns. Eventually Rommel was defeated and Italy became the next objective. Jim was involved in the beach landings at Pantelleria, where he collected some shrapnel from a Stuka attack. That shrapnel in time probably caused the cancer which afflicted him, but not until he had lived a full, active life, passing away at the age of 80. His convalescence was on the island of Capri, which I think he found quite agreeable, particularly in relation to the attention of the Italian nurses, perhaps. A photograph was later found in Jim's possessions of an Italian-looking lady who may have been one of those nurses.

I wrote the following poem after a visit to the Amalfi Coast where Vesuvius was clearly visible over the town Naples and Pompeii, which we also visited.

Volcano

A breeze, like a wet leaf across the forehead,
The lemon in my drink submerged in icy water,
The ice-cubes with zest amplify and reflect the bright March sunlight
Here by the bay of Naples.
Under a humid sky, the soft contours of Vesuvius across the water
Belie the deadly terrors the mountain visited upon Pompeii
Both destroyed and preserved by its fires.
And again in 1944 angered by obscenities of war rather than decadence
It fumed and raged
A beacon for bombers and fighters like my father upon the beaches of Anzio.
I am far away now; far, far away where nothing holds me, nothing controls me.
Hoping for a breeze to guide, or some hand to grasp or volcanic fire to burst.
A child's balloon drifting away with dangling string.
In the void of annihilation may something enduring be cast.

March 2008

My father didn't talk much about the war, but he did mention an event that had an effect on him. This was the battle at Monte Cassino. He recalled an incident which took place at night. An American plane wanted to land but the authorities refused to light up the landing strip for fear that this would help the enemy. He talked about how the American plane went back and forth searching unsuccessfully for the landing strip. Eventually it crashed into a hillside. All the aircrew was lost.

Later he was serving with an anti-aircraft battery when they were attacked by German bombers. The gun next to him went off and the force of it knocked him off the gun platform. However, he was determined to fire and scrambled back to his position. The slight delay resulted in his gun scoring a direct hit on a Junkers 88 bomber, which plunged to the ground, much to the satisfaction of the Italians working in a nearby factory, who rewarded his gun group with a cash prize.

Following the war, Jim demobbed with the rank of Lieutenant Colonel, but after a week back with the bank he decided civilian life was too tame. He re-enlisted in the Royal Army Ordinance Corps, and the Army became his career.

My mother was scarred by the war in different ways. In her late teens she fell in love with a violin prodigy called Desmond Mitchell. He was being coached by Madam Menges in London alongside Sir Neville Marriner, who later went on to lead the orchestra of St Martin's in the Fields. Her father was a farmer in Dunchurch, near Rugby, Warwickshire. He was a very enterprising man and one of the top sportsmen in the village. He negotiated for the land on which Dunchurch Cricket Club now stands. He also ran the Post Office, and the local dairy. My father's own father was evacuated to Dunchurch to avoid the bombing in London. This turned out to be a good move as his house in Wimbledon was demolished by a V2 flying bomb fired from France, resulting in the loss of his beloved double bass and his stamp collection.

My mother's father had fought in the First World War. Rather than joining the Warwickshire Yeomanry, he joined the Signals as he didn't want to be involved in taking horses to war. He was sent to Palestine, where they were engaged in fighting Turks. He wrote a short memoir of his experience of travelling to the Holy Land and the sights of biblical importance in his own exquisite handwriting, though he did not report on the conflict itself. He kept a couple of mementos, which included a Morse code handset which he kept on his desk alongside two beautiful bronzes of mounted knights in armour. He also kept the nose of a Turkish bomb, which he used as a doorstop. He was fortunate to be in an area where the fighting was less intense than the horrors of the Western Front and he escaped the war relatively unscathed. He was too old to fight in the Second World War, and as a farmer his role was deemed essential on the home front.

Nevertheless, the war came to my grandfather through a couple of incidents. His farm was near Coventry, which was a major target for the Germans because it was a centre of manufacturing. One day a bomb was dropped in one of his fields. The bomb failed to explode. Fearlessly he went into the field to rescue the livestock. Later in the day the bomb went off, leaving a huge crater in his field. Forever afterwards, that field was known as the Bomb Hole Field.

In a separate incident, a Spitfire was shot down following a dog-fight. It crashed in one of his fields and exploded. There was a horse in the field; though physically unharmed, the horse suffered shock and fell to the ground. It never got up again. Mary's father was a very energetic man, and he finally died of a heart attack in his own farmyard as he was helping to deliver a calf.

Dunchurch was an important village during the coaching era of the 18th century. The main coaching inn still stands, as the Dun Cow Hotel. Next to it stands a statue of Lord John Scott, who is attributed with preventing the railway coming through Dunchurch. The railway was diverted instead to Rugby, the birthplace of rugby football.

There is also a Norman Church, St. Peter's, where many of my family are buried including my parents. Just down the road from the church on former glebe land (land which formerly belonged to the church) stands Glebe Farm. My mother built this home on land left to her by her father, William Butlin. The remaining farmland and the original farmhouse, Laurel Farm, went to her brother Peter Butlin, who continued farming the land.

At Dunchurch

Dry and gnarled, dead-looking trees.
How can it be that these skeletons
Should still be conduits of life
To bud and blossom in beauty?
To the place where my roots are deep,
To where my father lies buried
To where the Barby Road in Spring

Is a road to memories of death
Is there a stirring in my tired heart?
Is there new warmth in my veins?
From this man new life can come
By the resurrection miracle
In the bright wonder of the frosty morning spring,
Where woolly sheep and curious foxes
Leave fresh footprints on the virgin grass,
And call me to have courage
In faith, in springtime wonder
Tired and drained I return
And his father too,
Amid the promise of life
That God alone creates,
And recreates
To step out again.

22.03.1995

My life as an expat has had many advantages. In particular, I have had the chance to access many different cultures and approaches to life and education. However, the major downside of an expat life is the sense of not knowing ultimately where you really belong. My godmother Beryl would be the opposite extreme to me. She was totally comfortable with her life in Warwickshire, which I believe she never left. Her husband had been very successful as the marketing manager for Rover. After he passed away, Beryl moved to a small sheltered housing development near the heart of Stratford-on-Avon. As I reflected on her life, I wrote this poem.

Godmother

So farewell dear Beryl, I remember you so well,
Family, friend and tennis courts and Cotswold village bells,
Your deep sense of permanence, England was yours,
I envied your belonging, my life took a different course.
Now older, reaching for fulfilment through my deeds,
Searching for true value, casting wide the seeds,
From Hong Kong to Belgium and stations in between,
Yet you possess what I have sought: an ever-running stream.
I watched the Avon flowing, the heart of your home town,
Turning blues to hope, could she turn me around?
Impart to me belonging, that deep sense of home?
Am I doomed to be a wanderer, restless and alone?
From cross to post to a pilgrim until my final days,
A self-invented character upon life's draughty stage.
Still I believe there is a home, I see it in my dreams,
A place of trust and knowing and flowing together of streams.

This sense of home may have influenced my mother, who persuaded her boyfriend Desmond to volunteer for the Royal Air Force even though he had exemption. Desmond was not so lucky. He was assigned the role of airgunner and was the tail gunner of a Lancaster bomber crew led by a New Zealander. On his 20th mission, over Germany, he was shot through the eye by a Messerschmitt 109. Of course he died instantly, though his plane was able to return to its base in Lakenheath, Suffolk safely.

In many ways, my mother never got over Desmond's death. She kept on display a picture of him playing violin and retained and re-read his letters throughout her life. She showed me one of the letters, in which he expressed his intention that they should be married. In some ways, the shock of Desmond's death and the feeling of guilt over having encouraged him to sign up sustained the romantic bond with this musical prodigy throughout her life. Sadly, this also created a cloud over her relationship with my father, who was clearly aware that he was a second choice.

Mary got to know my father through his father, who would visit the farmhouse to buy his milk and stop by for a cup of tea each morning. He would read Jim's letters from Africa and Italy and through this the family got to know him. Though Mary was twelve years younger than my father and turned him down a couple of times, they were eventually married at St Peter's Church, Dunchurch.

Immediately after the wedding Jim left for Hamburg, Germany, to take up the task of clearing war debris in the form of German trucks and equipment. Mary joined him a short while later and found the experience of leaving the comforts of home quite a shock. She became pregnant with her first child, Philip, who was born with a hole in his heart and died within a year. It took her some time to recover from this experience. My older brother Chris was born in 1950 and I followed in 1953, when my parents were relocated to the UK. They lived in the village of Salgrave, in Northamptonshire, which is the home of the Washington family. My birth was at Brackley Cottage Hospital, which still exists today.

The next posting was an interesting one. Jim was seconded to the Arab Legion in Jordan, which was led by General John Glubb, known as Glubb Pasha. He was a kind and thoughtful man and when he heard of my mother's interest in horses, he arranged for one of his to be sent around for my mother to ride, riding having been her main interest in rural Berkshire. This culminated in her buying a racehorse called "Jimmy Newbury".

Being very young, my memories of Jordan are limited to a few incidents. I remember seeing the cook boy catch a bird on the veranda with his bare hands, and being very impressed with my father's Arab headgear, which was augmented by the badge of the Arab Legion. When I was 14 my father gave me the cap badge, which I attached to a cap, wearing it Aussie style. I took it on a canoeing holiday, but one day an unexpected gust of wind blew it into the river Wye and it was gone forever. I lost his watch in a similar way on the same trip, which became a bit of a theme as later in my life when flushing the toilet my sparkling new Seiko watch became unbuckled and found its way into the sewage system. It is possibly still keeping time somewhere in the South China Sea.

The house we had in Jordan had a sunken garden. For Christmas I was given a beautiful present: a huge red Tonka truck. I made the mistake of leaving the truck in the garden, from which it disappeared. I caught sight of it a few weeks later - by now looking rather beaten up - under the arm of a Palestinian boy.

My father carried a Beretta pistol at this time as things were a little unstable politically. Much later, in England, I remember finding that pistol several years later in a chest of drawers in the garage where Jim kept his tools. Next to the pistol were a couple of clips of ammunition. That was a bit of a shock when I was just looking for a screwdriver. We disposed of the gun in the septic tank, where I guess it still remains.

The next posting was the Central Ammunition Depot, Bramley, near Basingstoke. The depot had a very good shoot and I have vivid memories of pheasants and hares hanging up in the pantry and having to be very careful when eating the cooked pheasant so as not to break my teeth on the shot. It was at Bramley that Mary's last child was born; this was Tim, who arrived in 1957.

My brother Chris was a redhead with a keen sense of adventure and irrepressible energy, which inevitably led us into trouble. He had an early fascination with fire and unwisely experimented with starting bonfires, which was heavily frowned upon, given the fact that we lived in an ammunition depot. This was the first and only time that I remember my parents pulling out a cane to whack us on the backside, a job in which my mother took the lead.

Another episode which I remember involved our neighbour Robert Jarman, who was about Chris' age. There was a large pile of wooden blocks which were to be used to fuel fires. Chris decided we should have a war with the blocks, using them as imaginary hand grenades. It was Chris and Robert against me. Unfortunately one of the blocks hit me on the forehead. With blood streaming from my head, my mother drove me to the depot hospital, where I received my first stitches. I bear the scar today.

A second scar that I acquired around the same time was inflicted unintentionally, I hope, by my father. He always carried a penknife, which he used for odd jobs from time to time. He had the bad habit of leaving the blade open and putting the knife in the top pocket of his jacket, with the blade protruding a few inches. He picked me up one day, after he had been using the knife, as a token of paternal affection. However when he came to put me down, he had forgotten about the knife, which cut a gash on the right side of my neck. Again the blood flowed and the scar still remains.

Since my mother and our housekeeper, who was called Agnes, were mostly preoccupied with Tim, I found myself with time to explore. I had a tricycle which made this simpler, and I think for the first time in my life I had a sense of loneliness, which was complemented by some kind of awareness of God. One day my parents asked me to take a lettuce from our extensive garden round to a neighbouring family. The family kindly rewarded me with some sweets. Following that, from time to time, on my own initiative, I would cut the largest lettuce I could find and take it over to the family with the hope of further reward in the form of sweets, which were invariably forthcoming.

At the time I went to a school called Sherbourne Hill where I formed a troop, comprising mainly girls, to practise marching and other military activities. The world of women was a bit of a mystery to me. I remember lying on my rug as part of the requirement to have a nap after lunch when a rather large teacher stepped over my head, affording me an unintended graphic illustration of her undergarments which included what I now understand to be suspenders and such like. At the time this was an inexplicable world to me, containing both shock and mystery.

I have never worn a wedding ring, and I put this down to one of my father's stories at Bramley. He told me that as a soldier, he had jumped off the back of a three-ton truck and as he jumped his ring got caught on a clip on the truck. He was dragged some considerable distance before he was rescued.

Bramley is also where I learnt to ride a bike. My underdeveloped skills led me to crash into rose trees, which scratched me up but increased my determination to improve my skills. I also remember seeing the gardener catch a rabbit by the ears before clubbing him on the back of the neck. This was a bit of a shock, but was later justified as being necessary in view of an outbreak of myxomatosis among the rabbit population. On a brighter note it was also the first time I was invited with my older brother to accompany the officer who worked for my father to the Mess, where we were treated to ginger beer and Mars bars.

The next news I heard was that we should be leaving for Hong Kong, where my father took up the post of Commander of the Royal Army Ordnance Corps. Accompanying us on the trip would be a Chinese girl whose main responsibility would be to look after the three children. She came to stay with us before we left and we found her uncomfortably strict. We picked damsons off the tree in the garden, and we were looking forward to a feast of fruit, but somehow she persuaded us to surrender our bounty on the basis that the fruit was not sufficiently ripe.

Before long soldiers crated up our belongings and we were on our way to Southampton docks to join SS *Nevassa* for the six-week journey by sea to Hong Kong. Life on board ship was very agreeable with the waiters and crew and their white starched uniforms, linen table cloths and silverware. We also stopped off at interesting places, the first of which was Gibraltar. This was where my image of monkeys changed from benevolent creatures to animals to avoid. The apes of Gibraltar turned out to be aggressive and unpleasant, and my opinion of them was not helped by putting my hand in some ape excrement, which was both very smelly and impossible to remove.

Sea trips seem to bring out romantic tendencies. I remember being on deck talking to a Scottish lady who must have been in her thirties. I was talking to her about my admiration for things Scottish, including the history and the tartan. I was only seven years old but I must have been saying the right things, because before I knew it she said, "I know what you want" and planted a big wet kiss on my lips.

One of the sorrows of the trip was that the family had decided to leave my older brother Chris with my grandfather in Dunchurch. They felt that education in Hong Kong might not be of a good enough quality. Chris never really recovered from being parted from the family at the young age of eight. He talks about being abandoned to this day, and he is now 64. One may argue that the decision paid off as he was offered a place at the elite Rugby School, where he relished its sporting opportunities.

Our next stop was Suez, where I remember my father bartering with traders who came alongside the ship. He bought an ebony elephant with ivory tusks. I remember when I was about 14 inexplicably painting the elephant white. It must have been at the time when I was developing an interest in pop art, thought I don't think my contribution did much to advance the genre.

Following Suez, we stopped at Aden and Colombo before finally arriving in Hong Kong.

From the word go, I found Hong Kong terribly fascinating. It somehow seemed larger than life, with constant movement, vitality and contrast. At that time, in the early sixties, the harbour was clean and the sky was clear. At the end of our first trip on the Star Ferry we saw a dozen boys calling to the passengers to throw coins in the water for them to dive for. I had never seen anything like it and in some ways felt a bit envious of them.

Here is a poem which captures some of the vitality of this dynamic city.

Hong Kong

Your dragons are in my blood,
They wake me in the night restless for the taste of jasmine,
Aching for the orange sun on the green sea
For a world illuminated by neon signs
Displaying characters which meaning nothing, yet so much.
Of rocky bays and rubbish strewn coves
And fruit like polished jewels, displayed for sale.
In the black evening swimming in the calm pool,
Looking back up at the thirty-storey block,
And views of the sunset smudged with ink,
The dying light, air-conditioned sleep,
Where the satisfied dragons now rest content
And my dreams can soar like the sea kites
Playful for walks on snaky paths
Across the backs of hills with views
Of villages where mongrels bark
Above the twinkling harbour.

CHAPTER TWO

LIFE IN HONG KONG

Hong Kong has always been a place of huge contrasts between rich and poor. My father's work included helping new refugees from China who were escaping the cultural revolution. Large numbers of these eventually created their own shanty towns and squatter villages in Hong Kong. From time to time, gas fires would explode or ignite the house, which led to massive fires and hundreds of squatters being made homeless. What was fascinating to me was the pride of the people, despite their poverty. The children going to school from these villages would always be immaculately turned out.

Another thing I admired about the Cantonese was their attitude to work. They were industrious and incredibly efficient. They clearly drew immense pride from doing their work well and quickly. Plus they had an amazing entrepreneurial spirit which together with the rule of law and with government assistance, enabled them to flourish and achieve their amazing commercial potential.

We were blessed to live at 129 Repulse Bay Road in a block called Royden Court, on the 10th floor. This afforded magnificent views of both the bay and the spectacular sunsets. I remember hearing a man in the apartment below us singing the hymn *Holy Holy Holy*. It was easy to see why he was so moved by the beauty of the scene.

Hong Kong was a very safe place and my younger brother and I were given a lot of freedom. Every afternoon we would make our way down to the sands of Repulse Bay beach. It was here that I taught myself to swim, pushing off the sand and flailing with my arms and legs until eventually I swam with a pretty incomprehensible stroke.

I realised after I got back to the UK that I couldn't swim in a straight line. At my next school I entered the swimming sports, but despite beating everybody at front crawl my route from one end of the pool to the other was a zig zag, which included knocking into the boy in the next lane. Consequently I was disqualified. Besides the ability to swim after my own fashion, I also acquired the most enormous blisters on my back. From then on I always wore a shirt for protection.

On a couple of occasions my parents' liberal approach may have been stretched too far. On one occasion they came back to find me and my brother sitting on the window ledge with the window open, ten floors up. We felt safe, but it caused them a bit of a panic. For another crazy escapade

Chris, my older brother, when he came out to visit us, climbed out of one window and made his way outside, walking along the window ledge and holding onto the fixed frame before re-entering the bedroom through the next open window. It was the most daring and crazy thing I have ever seen.

On another occasion Tim and I decided to act out the roles of American gangsters and we raided my father's cigar collection, taking a couple of puffs and having a verbal exchange in what we thought was an American accent and then stubbing the cigars out. My mother also felt safe enough to leave me and my brother in the Botanical Gardens for two hours each week while she went to a Chinese painting class. She gave me and Tim a dollar note each, which was enough to buy four ice lollies. So we measured out the time - one ice lolly for one half hour.

I spent a lot of the time watching the elderly Chinese men practising their Tai Chi, a wonderful ritualistic dance, like so many Chinese things dating back thousands of years. It combined a strange majestic power based on a clear understanding of the forces at work in the human body and how to bring these into balance. Fortunately my mother gained considerable ability with her Chinese painting and many of her birds and flowers still happily adorn the walls of her children's houses.

Chris was inaugurated as a member of the BOAC Junior Jet Club and travelled from England to Hong Kong on the new Comet 4 airliner. He may have cheated death again, as two of these aircraft crashed as a result of metal fatigue. When he joined us swimming at Repulse Bay beach, he felt a strange sensation on his foot and raised it out of the water, asking me if I could see anything. A crab had attached itself to his big toe. Always one for adventure, he started to swim out to the pontoons. Jetlag must have set in and I heard him shouting for help. Fortunately my father was near at hand and rescued him.

Chris' lively behaviour introduced me to the concept of looking for 'fag ends' as he put it, even though he was only about 10. He would light these up and take a couple of puffs until he burned his fingers. We would also race Dinky cars down the gutter of the steep drive down from our apartment. These would gather incredible momentum, and would inevitably fly. One found its way down the drainage grate, a minor tragedy of my early life.

I went to school initially at Victoria Infant School, which was situated inside Victoria Barracks. This area has now been developed into a complex of major hotels. I had a reputation at school for wrestling with other students and was seen as the prize fighter. What was curious to me was that rather than rebuking me for my behaviour, some of the teachers, if they caught other students fighting, would bring them to me for a wrestling contest. Somewhat bizarre, when I look back on it.

In due time I advanced to Victoria Junior School, which was also located at the Barracks (Hong Kong). We would usually go to school on an army transport bus, or occasionally they would bring a truck such as those used by the proper soldiers. It was always something that all of us hoped we would get a ride in. The bus escort was usually a soldier who had a broken arm or suchlike. This gave us the opportunity to study the different cap badges. My favourite was the 17th/21st Lancers, whose cap badge was the skull and crossbones with the motto 'Death or Glory'.

I had been given a pile of Superman comics by one of the officers at our quarters. Though the comics had a big impact on me from a graphic point of view, I offered to exchange them for the cap badge I described. The corporal took the comics and said he would bring the badge the next day. Unfortunately I never saw him again. It seemed that it was my destiny to be efficient in losing cap badges.

When I went to the junior school my father would often take me to school in his staff car. This was a model called a Vanwall and driven by Corporal Vernon, who, much to my fascination, appeared for duty one day with a massive love heart tattooed on his forearm. When my father questioned him about it, he said he had acquired it after a night revelling with comrades down in Wanchai. I was required to conceal myself in the footwell of the front seat when my father was dropped off at Wavell House, which was where he worked, before being driven off to my school. This place still exists, in what is now Hong Kong Park.

Hong Kong is a place of extremes; besides the crackling heat there are also enormous deluges of rain. At this time I developed an interest in building Airfix models. I tried out my model of the *Bismarck* during one of the storms at school. However, there was definitely a problem with stability and the ship was constantly overturning, breaking off bits of the infrastructure as it did so. I was nestled with my friend under a paper parasol, which survived about five minutes in the downpour.

At the school I had my first encounter with drama and

took part in a production. I never suspected that drama was going to play an important part in my early teaching career.

Looking back on it, living in Hong Kong at an early age had a huge impact on me, both as a place and also because of the power of Chinese culture. Everything was larger than life: the bugs, the banana tree leaves, the sunsets, the extravagance of the hotel buffets, the privilege of being a member of the colonial power, the incredible signs illuminated on Nathan Road at night, the boldness of Chinese calligraphy, the Chinese love for the colour red, and the sense of urgency as people moved about their business.

The other side of life was equally striking. I remember rows of homeless refugees sleeping on the covered sidewalks in Queens Road East. This was intimidating to me in its complete foreignness. However, we were blessed with an intermediary. His name was Tam Lok Sang, aka Tommy Tam, a civilian employee of the RAOC who reported to my father. He was the one who helped my parents buy jade ornaments and rosewood furniture and more importantly, he was the one who procured a kite for me.

I took the kite out to try it back at Royden Court, where I was joined by the caretaker. He was successful at getting the kite airborne, but before I had a chance to try it, it had inexplicably dived towards the ground and got caught in a bush. It was irretrievable.

I seemed to have a knack for offending some of the locals, not least our Chinese amah, Ah Ming. She got so irritated with me that she told my parents I had to change my ways or she would leave. Fortunately I had the sense to apologise, and pretty soon Ah Ming and I became good friends, which was just as well, as she was an excellent cook.

I also upset one of the caretakers during his lunch break. He responded by throwing pungent fish gravy over me. The smell was pretty overpowering and it took a good bath to get rid of it.

These incidents were early lessons in the importance of treating people with respect regardless of their situation in life.

I enjoyed going around the golf course with my father at Deepwater Bay, followed up by a lime soda and a swim in the ocean. However, our time in Hong Kong was drawing to a close. At the age of 50, my father took early retirement - apparently there were too many Lieutenant Colonels in the army. The cash inducement appealed to him and he finally planned to return to my mother's home in Warwickshire.

My mother and my younger brother Tim left first on board the troopship *Oxfordshire*. I stayed on for a few more months with my father. We were to return by plane. Jim took me to a parade in honour of Princess Alexandra. There were large contingents of troops on the parade ground, including some Gurkhas whose main duty was border control. For some reason Princess Alexandra was delayed and the sun began to take its toll. Soldiers began to faint in the heat, falling like dominoes. The Gurkhas were more resilient than the Europeans. Eventually the guest of honour arrived and the proceedings got under way. These kinds of events helped shape the idea in my mind that my future career would be as an army officer, following in my father's footsteps.

I was excited to go back to the UK on a Viscount airliner and the flight included a couple of stops for refuelling, one of which was at Istanbul. As I touched down at Heathrow, I remember saying "Good Old England". I had no concept of what would come next.

My father pictured himself as the bursar of a preparatory school in Dunchurch called Dunchurch Winton Hall. This was influenced by the fact that we were to live initially with my mother's father at his home, Laurel Farm, which adjoined the school via a small wood.

Staying at Laurel Farm was quite an adventure. I remember we returned in winter, which was quite a contrast to Hong Kong temperatures. I shared a bedroom with my older brother. I remember waking up to discover ice on the inside of the windows. Outside was the manure heap which was smoking and smouldering in the crisp morning air. Whilst we lived at the farm my father was having his house renovated in the next village, Thurlaston. My mother named the house Mill View. Though there was a mill in Thurlaston, we could never see it from our house.

My father did get a job at Dunchurch Winton Hall, but not as the bursar. He was given a job as a teacher of English, History and Geography. The school meant a lot to me. It was a much closer community that my previous school in Hong Kong.

By now I was much more aware of the importance of relationships. I discovered that my over-zealous interaction was not to everyone's taste. The school classes had about a dozen students and I would guess the entire school was not much over 100. The students were very pleasant. They came from privileged homes and besides me and my brother, they were all boarders.

Some of the teachers were a little eccentric. For example, we had a Latin teacher who was nicknamed

'Waffle' because he was very indistinct in his speech. He wore plus-fours and had nicotine stains on his moustache and fingers. He seemed a sad and lonely man.

One of the students complained to his parents about Waffle, and the next thing we knew he had been fired. His story had an even sadder conclusion, as he decided to hang himself in his apartment.

Another teacher I remember was called Harry Bland. His name was a bit of a misnomer, because his temperament was anything but bland. He certainly taught me that a teacher's temperament can have a huge effect on the learning of a child. I never liked mathematics very much, but it was Harry who sealed my lifelong aversion to the subject. When I was struggling to understand a concept, I would go up to the teacher's desk and ask for further explanation. At this, Harry would turn purple in the face and shout at me "I just explained that on the board there!" Naturally, knowing what his reaction was going to be to my pleas for my help, I decided not to make any inquiries when I got stuck. This resulted in my maths skills falling further and further behind.

I think it is important that a teacher maintains an even temperament. Children learn at different rates and have different skill sets. They must be treated with love and patience. When I came to my O levels some years later, I took 11 subjects, and maths was one of the two I failed.

However, I do owe Harry a debt of gratitude for including me in the cast of *Henry the IV part 1*, which the school performed in the local Women's Institute Hall. There is something magical about being involved in a production. My memory of that served as a spur for me in my later career, which included teaching drama. Sadly for Harry, he passed away when he was rather overly excited during a game of tennis. I believe he suffered a heart attack, and possibly his excitable nature was caused by undiagnosed hypertension.

Being one of the only two day boys in the school, after tea I would head towards my grandfather's house at Laurel Farm. This meant going through a wood, which on a winter's night in the dark was a little intimidating for a nine-year-old and a 12-year-old. It was comforting to hear the singing from the evening prayers. The piano students in the school would be asked which hymn they would like to learn to play. The funny thing was they all seemed to choose the hymn *Fight The Good Fight*. So with regularity, our walk through the trees would be accompanied by the strains of this hymn.

There was another teacher whom my mother corresponded over with someone who knew him from a previous job. I didn't understand the nature of their problem as a ten-year-old, but later on I understood that he had a reputation for interfering with young boys. The situation repeated itself at Dunchurch, and he too was removed. That is the worst thing that can happen at a school; it's a massive betrayal of trust.

I gained my second experience of corporal punishment at Dunchurch Hall. There was a prep period every evening and I completed my prep, then sneaked a sweet into my mouth. The prefect who was taking the prep session noticed it and reported to the headmaster. The result was 'six of the best' in the head's study.

I remember another encounter with the headmaster which resulted in him putting me on silence for tea. I was not supposed to converse with anybody during teatime. I was seated next to a boy called Holmes, who was extremely quiet. There was a prefect at the end of the table. I felt safe to talk because I couldn't figure out how the head teacher would know. However, at the end of tea he came over to the prefect and said "Did that boy talk?" looking at me but not mentioning any name. My heart sank, as I thought I was going to be visiting his study one more. However, to my amazement the prefect said "No, sir, he didn't talk". I was flooded with relief. After the head left I asked the prefect why he had said I hadn't talked and he replied 'I thought the head was pointing at Holmes', who had not said anything during the entire teatime.

Teatime was a strange affair. At the beginning of each term we had to bring several pots of jam to spread on our bread. We had to consume one pot in its entirety before we got the next pot. Of course, this became rather boring; one flavour only day after day until the pot was empty. Teatime was policed by the matron. I was in such a hurry to finish my jam that I put it on quite thick. She came over to me and said "We are being over liberal with the jam are we, Miller?" She told me to sit up straight.

The school had regular Christian worship and I remember to this day singing the songs with all my heart. A particular song that we sang was a moment of significance for me. The line that I remember is "Come to my heart, come to my heart Lord Jesus, there is room in my heart for thee". At that moment I felt again a connection with God in a way that transcends age.

Come To My Heart, Lord Jesus

Come to my heart, Lord Jesus;
Teach me to walk in your way.
Come to my heart, Lord Jesus;
Come to my heart today.
Give me the peace and joy
That only you can bring.
Come to my heart, Lord Jesus;
Give me a song to sing.

Fill me with love, Lord Jesus;
Teach me to walk in your way.
Fill me with love, Lord Jesus;
Fill me with love today.
Give me the peace and joy
That only you can bring.
Fill me with love, Lord Jesus;
Give me a song to sing.

Answer my prayer, Lord Jesus;
Teach me to walk in your way.
Answer my prayer, Lord Jesus;
Answer my prayer today.
Give me the peace and joy
That only you can bring.
Answer my prayer, Lord Jesus;
Give me a song to sing.

One thing I enjoyed a lot at school was the sport. I was immensely proud of my brother Chris, a natural sportsman. I remember him playing cricket, scoring three sixes off consecutive balls. I remember him throwing a ball at the stumps from the outfield. He put a spin on the ball so it landed right by the stumps and then smacked into them, running out the batsman. Sport is his passion in life and his greatest talent.

I also had my own success on the rugby field, at the age of ten playing for the under 13s team as the hooker. We played the other seven prep schools from the region, and generally we did pretty well.

One quaint habit of the school was to check on the bowels of each student in the morning. We would be marched to the toilets next to the gym and had to report if we had been successful or not. The truth was, there was no way the teacher could check on what we had reported. Generally if you said it was a tick rather than a cross, you could avoid being sent to the matron for medication or laxative.

The toilets had their own special names. The ones by the gym were called Cross Gym and the ones elsewhere were Cross Black. If you wanted to go to the toilet during a lesson you would raise your hand and say "Can I please go Cross Gym sir?" My number at school was 41, and my older brother was 69. These were the numbers of our pegs where our coats and bags would be stored.

Chris went from prep school to the prestigious Rugby School. He would ride his bicycle three miles to the school every day, rain or shine, wearing his red and white Townhouse cap. The caps the students wore denoted their houses and created a feast of colour as they changed lessons in the town. I rather regret the decision to do away with the caps in the late 60s.

My father was keen for me to go to the local grammar school, which had been founded in the 1600s by the same merchant who founded Rugby School. The school was named after him, and was known as the Lawrence Sherriff Grammar School. To improve my chances of success in the crucial 11-plus entrance exam, my father drilled me in past papers every day. When the day of the test came he gave me instructions to sit near an open window, to aid my cognitive processes. I duly obeyed his instructions. I was successful in getting entry to the school.

Lawrence Sheriff Grammar School

Another problem of children who have lived abroad is that they have had experiences that most people cannot be privileged to enjoy. I found this in particular when I went to Lawrence Sheriff Grammar School. Most of the boys had little experience outside of Rugby, and this created a void between me and them in my mind, which led to a feeling of alienation which I felt during most of my time at the school. This phenomenon is now described as the 'Third Culture Kid Syndrome'. At the time, it was a substantial issue to deal with and led me to become quite reflective as a young person. The following poem to some extent tries to capture this dissonance.

You will find me between the idea and its expression

Between the impulse to kiss and the meeting of lips,
On the cusp of blue and green as the water drips,
As it glints in the sun through the cracked church door,
As the quest for the meaning of existence begins,
Between shaping the question and offering solutions,
Between hope and regret, the now and forever,
Between dreams and reality, hope and despair,
In the space between us, in what should have been said,
Where love fills the void between the living and dead.
(Where love fills the void and its passion burns red)
Before it falls down onto the flagstone floor,
Before moisture on the forehead fades away,
And echoes still ring from the words we pray,
Between noble ideals and our sad secret sins.
Exploring the context and forming conclusions.
As we walk alone, or step out together,
Passion and restraint, you'll find me there,

I link this experience to a certain of amount of shyness in my nature which, over time, I overcame. It also made me more self-sufficient, which in turn intrigued some people who felt they wanted to understand me better. As Arch Marchant said at university, 'Nick Miller: Man or Myth?" I think too much self-reflection can lead to over-introspection which to an extent can breed a degree of depression. I think this sentiment, linked with my keen interest in the blues, which by nature is a somewhat self-pitying genre, encouraged a melancholy mood, and the poetry and life of John Keats, who is my favourite poet, contributed to, at times, a lonely outlook. I overcame this kind of sentiment only after I had been teaching for a few years and married my pretty wife.

The following poem addresses some of these issues.

Hope

My words you translate, you do not hesitate
To explore the hidden places they are coming from
You gladly paid the toll at the drawbridge to my soul
The source of my emotions and the key to all the songs,
The questions of my life, you laid them all bare,
The public and the private, the hope and the despair.
To my heart you keep returning, again and again
A moth to a flame, there's something draws you on,
A stronger force than fear is pulling us both near
Like soulful sailors swimming to the siren's song.
I see love's fire illuminate and offer liberty,
Will its smoke conceal the entrance to eternity?
Thinking 'bout the situation, I feel a new sensation,
Like Moses, when he stumbled onto holy ground,
In the dawn's rosy glow I mumble words I do not know
And in the velvet darkness I can sense you all around,
This mystery half holy steals my aching heart away.
I chase the flames at night and follow clouds by day
I wake to angels singing, new inspiration bringing,
The sound of music drifting is leading me to where
There's stables and a manger, threats of evil, danger,
Where a baby's birth is contradicting my despair,
I'm falling on my knees, I'm worshipping a star
New love and inspiration are exploding in my heart.

Lawrence Sherriff was an all boys' school and coming from a family of three boys and no girls, it gave me a somewhat abnormal socialization. However, it did have excellent teachers and a strong emphasis on academics. I continued my interest in sport, playing rugby twice a week in winter and horse riding and cricket in the summer. My most successful sport was probably basketball. In rugby I sustained a few injuries, the most spectacular of which when I was playing full-back against Rugby School. The opposing centre three-quarter was approaching at high speed and there was just me between him and the try line. I don't know whether it was deliberate or not, but his knee met my face with immense velocity. The next I heard was the referee saying "I don't think he is quite with us yet". I had been knocked out and for weeks afterwards displayed an amazing spectacular bruise on my face.

Friends

Throughout my life I have been blessed with some amazing friends. These for the most part have been long-term relationships that I still enjoy today. The first of these was with a boy called Nicholas Davidson. We had in common a passion for the army. We were about 10 years old. At that point I saw myself following my father's footsteps into the army when I left school. Nicholas had built a kind of tank with a gun turret on top and room for one person inside, so either he or I sat inside and steered the tank while the other pushed. We set out on many dawn patrols, always hoping that we might discover some World War Two relics, though we never did.

At secondary school I formed an immediate bond with Richard Coss, which I will describe later. I also developed a friendship with Glyn Turner. He lent me my first guitar, which became a huge passion in my life. We would enjoy jam sessions in Guy Fawkes House, his home in the centre of the village of Dunchurch, which is where, in 1605, two of the Gunpowder Plot conspirators were arrested. We went on a number of Crusader camps and this was the start of me leading worship. Glyn would play his 12-string and I would sing and play the harmonica.

At university my brotherhood was with Jerry Akehurst, who was an outstanding acoustic guitar player and songwriter. He encouraged me to write my songs, which I have continued to do to this day. So far I have produced five CDs. I wrote many poems and produced a series of paintings as well as a book of short stories.

Jerry and I were part of a very close fellowship at Waveney Terrace. The group was very caring and we met each evening for prayer and to share our songs and food. Some students joined us, deciding to become Christians after what they saw in our fellowship group.

Whilst at university we started a fellowship at All Hallows Hall, which we called the Ark. At that fellowship I met two fanatical bass players. One was just fourteen years old, and his name was Gordon O'Byrne. At that time he was into Glen Hughes and bands like Uriah Heep and Deep Purple. He has been a consistent friend since that time. I remember visiting him in Tokyo, where he had made up his mind that he wanted to live. He has done just that, marrying a terrific Japanese girl called Kyoko.

I went to see him because he had a serious growth in his throat which they said could kill him before the age of 40 and he was about to go to hospital for an operation to see what they could do. Half way through the procedure the doctor changed direction with the surgery taking a more aggressive and radical route. Since then the throat has not been a particular concern and he plays bass on several of my recordings as well as designing the album artwork, making use of his talents as a graphic designer.

In my suitcase I took a bottle of whisky as a gift for Gordon. When I was stopped by Customs, the officer asked me to open my case. At that point we realised that the whisky bottle had broken and the contents had spilled all over my leather jacket and clothes. When I arrived at Gordon's house he was very disappointed at the demise of the whisky, but he said my whisky-scented clothes would do wonders for my reputation in Tokyo.

The second bass player was Malcolm Jackson. He had very fine features and very long straight blonde hair and for a while I genuinely could not make up my mind whether this was a girl or a boy. He was also extremely quiet and sat on the floor with a very straight back as if he was a dancer. Later on I discovered that he was a very serious bass player and completely hooked on Led Zeppelin. Malc and his wife Rosie have been close friends ever since.

Finally I will mention another friend from this era. This was Tony Lee, a Londoner, who joined our fellowship, the Ark, later. Years later he moved to Perth, Australia, where he was a successful Maths teacher. Tony continues to visit me today. We reconnected after some years when he was living in Thailand.

After I finished university we developed some close friendships in our new church, which was called St Mary Magdalene. The chief of these friendships was with twins, Peter and Paul Lefevre, who were plumbers. Our theology differed, but that didn't seem to matter and Peter remains a strong friend to this day. We invited them to be godparents to our first two children. They had a high church background - "smells and bells", they used to call it. This branch of the church seemed to breed people with a faith that was down to earth but also very practical in application. Every Sunday morning they would ferry pensioners or disabled people to their service, and they would lend their building expertise to developments of the church property, such as the new church hall, where we met for breakfast after Holy Communion.

Some people there didn't take to my guitar playing, feeling that it intruded on the solemnity of the service, and they referred to the guitars as 'them banjos'. But overall the community was warm and caring, and we felt very much at home at St Mary Magdalene, so much so that I named my rock group Magdalene, and our first baby was named Madeleine. This was also because of the Bible story where Mary Magdalene broke the alabaster jar of perfume over Jesus' feet.

After we moved to Hong Kong my closest friend became John Snelgrove. Beside our fun in leading worship together with our group Island Praise, we shared a similar taste in rock music, particularly the band Free. I was a big fan of Paul Kossoff, the guitar player in Free. I also became close friends with Jym Kay, who hailed from Chicago. He was the drummer of the band Citybeat and later we played together in other bands. I once stood in for the guitarist of Citybeat and was asked to report to the Landmark, which is one of the most prestigious shopping centres in central Hong Kong. It was not until we had finished the gig that Jim told me that we had been live on the radio. I hope I didn't make too many mistakes on my Les Paul guitar. Also from our Island Praise group I was close friends with Stephen Russell Smith, who was a banker. He was a flute player with a beard and he wore Jesus sandals. When I first met him I thought there was nobody less likely to be a close friend of mine, but his kindness and leadership together with his lovely wife Hillary changed my mind and we met with them regularly for tea at weekends for 18 months, until he went back to the UK, to Hammersmith, London, which must have been quite a contrast to Hong Kong.

When I moved to Belgium I became close friends with Terry the pastor, who I will say more about later. I also had immense respect for our school director, Joe Doenges, from the Lone Star state. He used to say 'Never ask a man if he is from Texas. If he is, he will tell you anyway, and if he isn't you don't want to embarrass him yourself!'

Back in Hong Kong we resumed our old friendships with close links with members of my last school leadership team, particularly Dion Chen, who was my right hand man, and Andy Higgins, who was completely dedicated to seeing the school thrive.

I think I have been amazingly blessed with great friends all my life. When I got sick in 2013, many of these friends travelled from as far away as Hong Kong and America to see me in Singapore, not to mention the support we received through email and social media.

Collections

I have always enjoyed making collections of various things that I find intriguing or beautiful. As a teenager I made a collection of bubble gum cards featuring great racehorses, the Second World War and the American Civil War. I also made a collection of toy cars which I still have today. As we grew more prosperous I was able to buy pens, which I considered beautiful, and these were an inspiration in writing poems and lyrics. Perhaps the crowning glory of my collection is the approximately 30-strong guitar collection featuring mostly Gibson and Fender guitars, plus three handmade Firebirds, which were made for me by the immensely talented Steve Lawrence whom I also knew from university days.

I've always been fortunate with my friends, and at various times in my life I've had particularly close male friends. At the Lawrence Sheriff Grammar School I met a fellow student called Richard Coss, mentioned above. We bonded immediately over music. These were the days of Jimi Hendrix and Cream. I had begun to learn the blues harmonica and graduated to the guitar at the age of 16, courtesy of my friend Glyn Turner, who lived in my village.

I became fascinated with Hendrix and Clapton, not to mention The Who. Richard's taste was pretty well identical to mine and we would meet up at break times or after school and play the harmonica and sing Hendrix tunes. We would even adapt them to certain situations, for example, when we were both playing centre three quarters in our own rugby team, when we got the ball we would sing "acting funny but I don't know why, excuse me while I score a try", which is adapted from the lyrics of Hendrix's 'Purple Haze'.

Richard's home life was not happy. His parents had been divorced and he didn't get on well with his dad. He didn't help the situation by taking his dad's car out, even though he didn't have a licence, and crashing it. Things deteriorated even further when his dad got a new girlfriend who had two daughters. His father accused Richard of being in a compromising position with one of the girls, which Richard said he wasn't.

It was winter leading up to A level exams, which would determine whether or not we would get into university. Richard came in one day with a broken nose; initially he told me he had slipped on the ice but later he confessed his father had thumped him in the face. Richard's world was falling apart and he was in no shape to take his final exams. Consequently his grades were not good enough to get to university. This was another influential factor in my later career as an educator. I realised that students could not perform academically unless their emotional needs were met. Consequently I became an advocate of strong pastoral care systems in schools.

I was always fascinated by Richard's interest in the railways. He had records of locomotives slipping on the rails, and so forth. Later on he did get a job on the railways but ended up a carpet salesman in Rugby. Life had not been kind to Richard.

I was living abroad. Just before moving from Hong Kong to Belgium I visited Rugby, and went to the post office. This was the summer of 2000. The manager of the post office was another schoolmate of mine. He saw me come in and came over to see me. He said "Have you heard about Richard?"

I said "No, what's happened?"

He said that the day before, Richard had parked his car by the railway tracks, taken a hose from the exhaust, put it through the driver's window and taken his life. His suicide note said "Wish me luck, today is the first day of the death of Richard Coss".

Goodbye Richard

I have kissed your lips,
How sweet the adventure of youth.
The mission burned so strong,
The anticipation of impact on a dreary world,
Armed with the belief that friendship was our transcending force,
Stronger than the steel sinews of a thousand years' history.
I could have told you it is not unusual to be bought by the world,
It happens every day – no cause for despair.
That blood has been shed to save you the pain of shedding yours.
Now you are gone and I am incomplete.
We inhaled the cynicism of maturity,
The compromise came on,
We blended in with the systems,
Too weak to change prescription's course.
Why didn't we have that last conversation?
To seek silver instead of salvation.
Yes, if you were here now I could tell you
A widow grieves, children cry,
Now what?
And I feel such loss
For the sake of that last missed conversation.

CHAPTER THREE

GRAMMAR SCHOOL, GUITARS & GOD

Besides sport, my main interests at grammar school were English and Art; both of these subjects were taught by teachers who would dress elegantly and have passion for their subjects. These are two more features that I emulated in my own career. I have always worn a suit and I've always believed that it is passion for the subject and a love for the students that become the compelling elements for inspirational teaching.

In Art, my favourite genres were pop art and op art. At the time, my mother was studying for her Art A level, and would play tapes explaining the theory behind the movements. Consequently I developed a lifelong interest in the work of Roy Lichtenstein, Andy Warhol, Jasper Johns and others. On the English side, I felt a strong affinity for John Keats, particularly his Odes and the idea of negative capability. I also favoured the other Romantics such as Shelley, Coleridge and Wordsworth. William Blake was a genius visionary.

Despite my respect for the school, by the time I had completed my O levels I had become weary of the environment and decided that if I was unsuccessful in my A levels I would join the army and follow my father's footsteps through officer training. I went for an interview at a couple of universities, but it was the University of East Anglia in Norwich that I connected with the most. I had recently been on a sailing holiday at the Isle of Wight, which I had thoroughly enjoyed. In the university handbook there was a picture of sailing boats at UEA. This influenced my choice.

I decided I would like to study English, but with additional subjects. I was interested in America, so I applied for English and American studies. My interview was conducted by a historian called Howard Temperley. He sent me a handwritten note after the interview saying that he was going to make me a low offer because he very much wanted me to join the university and that I should not think the university was a weak institution on the basis of setting me low grades to achieve. Fortunately, I did make the entrance requirements that he set for me and UEA became my next destination.

I had been going out with a girl called Jane between the ages of 14 and 16. I met her at a party arranged by one of my friends. She was a very feisty northerner. Her father was an engineer from Lancashire. The first time I called her she told me that she wouldn't go out with me until I had broken up with the girl I was seeing, Elizabeth, who was the daughter of a doctor. I had been going out with Elizabeth for six months. Elizabeth was my first girlfriend since the age of seven, when I was in Hong Kong and walked hand in hand with a girl called Susan whose father worked in the Army Pay Corps. She was six. One day I went around to her house and her mother invited me to visit her and her sister in the bath tub. This was when I got my education in the difference between boys and girls.

I was very attached to Jane; however, her father had to move to Cheshire for his work, and that ended the romance.

Parallel to this, I was on my spiritual journey. When Jane left, I would spend hours sitting beside the pond near my house reflecting on the meaning of life and the kind of person I wanted to be. It seemed to me that Jesus possessed all the admirable qualities that one could aspire to. I got more serious about attending the Church of England Youth Group called Crusaders, which met at the home of Glyn's parents, Pam and Barry Turner. They lived in a half-timbered Elizabethan house which had once been a coaching inn. This inn was where the Guy Fawkes conspirators, Robert Catesby and friends, were to have gathered had Guy Fawkes been successful in blowing up Parliament. Consequently the house was called Guy Fawkes House.

Glyn had lent me a guitar and I started almost immediately to write songs. Each Saturday my father would put on his tape recording of the radio programme 'My 100 Best Tunes'. He had a huge passion for music and when I came downstairs having been woken by the noise, I would see him conducting an imaginary orchestra. At this point I felt very little affinity for classical music but I felt a huge connection with the blues; people like Freddie and BB King, Peter Green, Fleetwood Mac, Jean Jac and other blues bands. Though Glyn and I were not very skilful, we had a great time taking turns playing drums or electric guitar. We played in one of the rooms at Guy Fawkes House.

I went to London to buy my first guitar, a Burns short-scale jazz guitar which looked very much like a Fender Stratocaster. We built speaker cabinets, trying to make them look like Marshall stacks. These we kept in my parents' garage, which was about half a mile away from Guy Fawkes House and St Peter's Church which were in the middle of the village. One day my parents went out shopping. I strapped on my Burns guitar, plugged it into the amplifier and turned it up to the maximum volume. Then I started blazing away at my poor renditions of blues classics.

Later on my mother came and told me that the Vicar had been trying to call her; he had been conducting a funeral in the graveyard and said I had been making enough noise to wake the dead. Part of me thought he should be grateful!

Besides blues and rock, Glyn and I played praise and worship music for the weekly Crusader meeting and also on Crusader camps that we attended in Dorset, Switzerland and the Isle of Wight. Glyn's parents asked me if I would like to go on holiday with them down to Somerset. I accepted the kind invitation, imagining more fun with Glyn. I didn't realise that this trip would have such an amazing impact on my spiritual journey.

When it came to Sunday, they piled us in the car and said we were going to church. I imagined this would be a

Church of England service similar to those I had experienced most of my life. I was wrong. To begin with, they drove 50 miles, which suggested to me that it must be some kind of special church. We finally arrived in the village of South Chard. We walked into the church, which was a non-traditional structure. I was amazed to see that the place was completely packed with a healthy proportion of young people. There was an incredible air of expectancy.

A lady walked down the aisle and I was told she was called Aunty Mill. She was married to Uncle Sid, who was the leader of the Chard Full Gospel Church. The worship erupted at tremendous volume and with huge conviction, which you could see written on the faces of the congregation. I had never seen anything like this before. You could see people fully believe that they were communicating with a God who heard them and who had a relationship of love with them.

Andrew Culverwell was leading the worship, singing from the piano. Then Harry Greenwood stood up to preach. He started giving out words of knowledge, saying things like 'Somebody here cannot move their arm. Come forward! Somebody has a pain in their left leg. Come forward!' Then he would lay hands on them and pray for them and then they were healed. I had read about such things in the Acts of the Apostles and in the letters of Paul, but I had never seen such things actually happen. It had a profound effect on me.

I was baptised in the river at Tarr Steps by Pam's husband, Barry. This experience has fuelled my religious convictions ever since. I wrote the following poem out of this sense of God's love for me and for all creation.

The language of love

A balm that evaporates before it can be applied.
How to calculate the value of what cannot be bought or sold,
How deceitful are the markets that fail to put a price,
Let this limited expression be the jar that shatters,
Let it be as substantial as the wind that blew your boat across the lake,
As compelling as the emotion that made a way to forgive me,
I am learning to speak the language of love
To understand, and ready to be understood.
Feeling more than I can express,
The nightingale that can't yet sing.
My love for you is bottled up,
It's like a colour I cannot describe,
How to make the spirit evident,
On the most prized and enduring commodity,
Blindly I break my clumsy words at your feet.
Perceive the aroma that it contains.
As soft as your breath on the voyage of sleep,
As radiant as the sunset's last moments of light,
When my heart was ice towards yours.
For such is love.
Let this limited expression be the jar that shatters,
Let it be as substantial as the wind that blew your boat across the lake,
As compelling as the emotion that made a way to forgive me,
Blindly I break my clumsy words at your feet.
Perceive the aroma that it contains.
As soft as your breath on the voyage of sleep,
As radiant as the sunset's last moments of light,
When my heart was ice towards yours.
My vocabulary is limited still,

But somewhere in my inadequate expression
Speaks an imperfect man's thanks for a perfect one's love.
May that be the scent that lingers when the last word has been spoken.

Pam and Barry had a nanny called Ruth King, employed to help look after Lucy, whom the family had adopted. She was clearly very comfortable with what was going on, but I couldn't get my head around it. I asked her 'What is it? What causes this difference?' She said "It's the Holy Spirit, just ask God". I kept asking her questions each day. Her answer didn't change: "Just ask God".

I was sharing a bedroom with Pam and Barry's future son-in-law, John. I knew that John was very sceptical about the happenings at the church. I lay on my bed in the darkness and prayed a very simple prayer. I just said "God, I don't understand this but I trust you anyway". At that point it seemed like a big wall of fire exploded in my stomach and coursed through my whole body. Then I felt a sensation in the back of my tongue and found myself speaking in a language I didn't understand. I knew that John was uncomfortable with these kinds of manifestations, so I left the room and went to find Pam or Barry. Pam told me that I had been baptised with the spirit and been given the gift of speaking in tongues. This was the most radical spiritual experience I had ever had, or have had since.

I started to attend house church meetings led by Ruth King's father, Den. These were in the same style as the Chard meetings. We shared my experience with my mother, who had been feeling quite stressed about her experiences with the local Anglican church. She also started to attend meetings with me and felt really encouraged by the more personal experience of my church. The church put on a special meeting for a visiting evangelist called David Greenow, who had prophetic gifts.

Of course I was contemplating my future, as I was about to leave for university. David came over to me during the meeting and said that I would have a ministry with young people. As I look back I can see that he was entirely correct. He didn't know me from Adam; he had never met me before. Amazing!

Soon the time came to leave for university. As I was on the train I sensed that God was speaking to me, saying he was going to use me for his purposes. I found myself in accommodation in a place called Waveney Terrace. It turned out that there were a number of Christians in the block and we started to meet each evening.

We became a strong community in our own right. There was an amazing bond of love between us and soon we found others who wanted to join us and become Christians also. This was the most powerful community experience of my life. Each evening God would give us some kind of word of encouragement and I found my next best friend. This guy, Jerry Akehurst, was an amazing guitar player and wrote terrific songs. We became musical soul mates; he encouraged me in writing my own songs and I encouraged him. Our music became the soundtrack for our fellowship.

My group of friends at the university was very tight and we enjoyed exploring Norfolk, particularly the coast, in my friend Sally's Renault 4. When it came to the Easter holiday in the first year, I joined with a group from the university who were involved with an evangelist called Eric Delve. Some time later, Eric became an Anglican clergyman.

However, his earlier life was a little different. He had been both a fireman and a male escort.

The idea was to reach out to people in the town where our university was located to share the gospel. I immediately became very close friends with Eric. Things at home were rather difficult for him as his wife had been in rehab and their relationship had been very strained. He became another of my close life-long friends and spoke at both my wedding and our 25th wedding anniversary.

At that time, we were wearing hippy-type clothes – Afghan coats, velvet jackets and enormous flares.

Following that outreach, I started a city-wide youth fellowship with a girl called Annie whom I met during the outreach. We called the fellowship "The Ark" and we met in the old hall of All Hallows Church. This was the church where Mother Julian of Norwich had her cell. She was the author of "Revelations of Divine Love", the Christian classic. Our fellowship grew very quickly; it was focused on contemporary prayer and worship, which allowed me to develop my guitar skills. I bought a Fender Shenandoah 12-string guitar on hire-purchase. That guitar is now a classic and I still have it.

When it came to the summer, Eric asked me to join him for some street pre-evangelism in London. This was prior to a big Christian event called Spree'73. We met at the Salvation Army Rink Club on Oxford Street. Eric had also invited friends from other places, including the fledgling London Youth With A Mission and the Froebel College in London, a teacher training college. It took a little while for the group to gel, mainly because Eric's relationship with his wife was going through a particularly difficult phase.

However, Eric had a bigger plan in mind; he wanted me to meet one of his protégés from Froebel. This was the leader of the Christian Union, a girl called Alison.

I first saw her in a church called Kensington Temple, a famous Elim church. Eric pointed Alison out to me and I realised what a beautiful girl she was. She had long dark hair with a fringe and a most glorious complexion. Her face was totally without blemish, with lovely features and a tapering chin like a woman in a Modigliani painting. I instantly felt drawn to her. She liked to wear long Indian-style dresses. Her favourite two were in dark green and dark pink. She wore a green Afghan coat which she told me she had emptied several bottles of perfume onto to improve the smell!

The parallels in our lives were quite amazing. Her father worked in senior administration in the Ministry of Defence Air division, the RAF. My father was an Army officer. She was the middle one of three girls; I was the middle one of three boys. When I was in Jordan, her family was in Aden, South Yemen. When my family went to an army posting in Hong Kong, she went to an RAF posting in Singapore. The similarity of our backgrounds no doubt was a factor in our feeling a wonderful sense of compatibility.

I continued my interest in songwriting and in poetry, and Alison was quite an inspiration. I include one of the songs I wrote for her at this time.

Moonbell

In a moment of true light the moon sounded like a bell
The evening star grew misty bringing tears to my eyes as well
and as the night blew in adoration

of a failed morning, a despairing queen
and if I were with her now,
I would sing unto her this sweet love dream
Moonbell ringing in my heart
Moonbell we will never part
Moonbell from the very start
Moonbell, moonbell
As I stand beside her memories of the loves of the day worn past
In an attitude of prayer my heart to hers inevitably is cast
And of all her gentle motions of her hand upon my own
For all I am is hers and I will with all my being give the finest things at my command
That she might happier live
So now as always as the nightbell tolls
I think of my lady fair, of her velvet words and eyes and the expression of her dew soft hair
And of her gentle motions of her hand upon my own
And so I offer her my heart for her to take it as her own,
As her own.

The next day, we met up at the Rink Club. I went alone because Eric's domestic situation was not going well, and asked the group to pray for Eric and his family. Alison tells me this was the turning point for her, as she had been a little annoyed by my joking with Eric. By the second day I met Alison, I knew she was going to be very special to me. Within a month, I asked her to marry me. I was 19 years old.

A Thousand Times Yes

You told me, 'a thousand times yes!',
With your conservative ways and your hippy dress
No make-up, no ruse, no lies, no pretence
Vulnerable, innocent, your soul made sense
Able to trust, you made it easy to dare,
Clear hazel eyes, Cleopatra hair
Clearest complexion, childlike smile
Uncalculating ways, undemanding style
The moment had come, we put our faith in fate,
So strong our belief, so why hesitate?
In an old Norfolk church, married in July
The bride wiped a tear from her father's eye.
The years have passed, many factors have changed
Save how this same strong impulse remains
Was the girl I love then the girl I love best?
I'll use your refrain, 'a thousand times yes!'

June 2012

Her engagement ring arrived to coincide with the *Daily Telegraph* announcement of our engagement on her birthday, December 22nd. Since we both had two more years of college left, we decided to postpone the wedding until the summer we finished school, in 1975.

When I told my parents about my intentions, they were confounded. My dad said, "You haven't earned a penny yet." He was asking how I was going to sustain a marriage with no experience of work. Work was honestly the last thing on my mind, and we went ahead and got married in the July after we had both graduated.

In many ways my father was a difficult and unreasonable man; I always put this down to the scars of war. However, there was no doubt in my mind that he loved us three boys and was proud of us. I remember him referring to the fact that all three of us had university degrees. But he could be very controlling. For example, Chris wanted to study oceanography, but Jim enrolled him at Sheffield Polytechnic for a surveying course which to this day is his profession. I have no doubt that he also had the potential to be a professional sportsman. The pinnacle of his achievement in this area was to play for England schoolboys at hockey.

Another example of my father's unreasonableness was that he said I could not get married in our local parish church. I actually think he did not want me to leave home as I was his main confidant, particularly in relation to his disputes with my mother. Interestingly I was also my mother's confidant in regard to her relationship with Jim. Often their main point of connection was to pick on one of us boys, usually over the meal table, and this would erupt in an emotional tirade. Anything could trigger this emotional catharsis. The best strategy was to keep a low profile.

Though I was disappointed that I wouldn't be married in our family church, the bright side was that we could be married in Norwich, which was where we had the majority of our friends. We were married in Winfarthing, near Diss in South Norfolk. The vicar of Winfarthing, Geoffrey Darrah, had become a particular friend. He offered to hold the wedding in his church. To meet Church of England requirements, I had to live in the parish for three weeks prior to the wedding. He invited me to stay with them in the vicarage. They were a delightful family of six children, and I passed the time mainly doing gardening work for them.

The wedding itself was a beautiful event. It was a soft, warm summer's day and the sun streamed through the church's pink glass windows, casting a soft pink light over all. The church was packed and our friends from the Ark and further afield sang with gusto. Our hymns were 'Alleluia Sing to Jesus', which is still my favorite hymn, and 'Morning has Broken'.

Following our reception in Eye, Suffolk, we set off on our honeymoon. I booked up five star hotels in Lincoln, Perth, Nairn - where we had our own turret in a castle - and a golf club in Oban.

I remember an incident that took place while we were in the Highlands. Our Vauxhall Viva got stuck in a narrow valley and a farmer pulled it out with his tractor. "What d'ya think ye're doin' doon here in a carr like thaat?" he said. A tractor was a better idea.

On the journey back to England we stopped in Edinburgh and Carlisle. As we came off the motorway on our return journey near my parents' home, the gearbox on our trusty Viva gave up the ghost. But it had been a great adventure.

CHAPTER FOUR

TEACHING, AND A NEW LIFE IN HONG KONG

Alison had already obtained a teaching position in Norwich, but I was less clear about my direction in life. Alison suggested that I should train to be a teacher. This thought had never occurred to me, as I thought my future would lie with rock-and-roll music. By this time, I had acquired a Fender Stratocaster, using some of the money left to me by my grandfather. It was a memorable day when we travelled to Ealing to purchase the coveted gift. It remains the most precious guitar of the collection.

I was still strong friends with Jerry, and we were planning to put a band together. The name of the band was Magdalene and we played in a variety of pubs in the

Norwich area. I was still very interested in songwriting, and we used quite a few original numbers.

I took Alison's advice and applied for teacher training college at the nearby Keswick Hall, which was affiliated to Cambridge University. During the interview, I was asked to explain what the Ark fellowship was about. Struggling to find a reference point, I said it was similar to the Christian Union at the college. The lady who was interviewing me reacted very strongly against this. I said, "It's a very open, welcoming sort of place where anybody could feel free to participate." She replied, "The Christian Union is anything but open and welcoming." And with that, I could see that my application was not destined to succeed.

I was determined to achieve some success, so I got myself a job at Colmans' food factory, which was near the river. My job initially was to run the production line for Robinson's orange juice. My tasks on the line varied between putting out the bottles, putting the tops on and putting the full bottles into the boxes ready for shipping. Eventually, I progressed to the night shift, doing a cleaning job, which was better paid. The night shift had earned a bad reputation; there was a leisure cruiser called the *Broads Princess* that passed by the factory along the river on its way out to the Norfolk Broads for evening entertainment. Some bored colleagues decided to bomb the boat with 2-litre bottles of orange juice, which did not go down very well with the management. Certain people inevitably lost their jobs. One had the satisfaction of having created a legend.

After a few weeks at Colmans', another job opportunity came my way. We were certain, upon reflection, that this kind of factory work was some people's most terrible experience of working life. It caused me to reflect on a career in education. There is so much potential in people that is so often unrealised. This became another lesson for me as a future educator and one of the things that has been a guiding force in my engagement with people. I tell them they should set themselves targets and goals and fulfil their potential, not sell themselves short. The single most important goal of a school is to enable students to fulfil their potential and live a full, happy, creative, satisfying life.

The job I was offered was something I was completely unprepared for. I was invited to be the manager of the Edmund Norvic Press, a printing company that specialized in printing documents for churches, particularly parish magazines. Little did I know that working at the Press would give me valuable experience in developing a pattern of work which would characterise my later career in educational reform.

The first thing I did was to reorganize the workflow through various machines we had in order to make production more efficient. The press had been operating at a loss. Happily, by the end of it we were in profit. A big part of my role was to do the graphic design and layout. This was before computers had come in and we were using cube-setting and Letraset. I enjoyed the graphic side of the job, as I had a strong affinity for graphic arts. Well, I certainly could have done with some expert training! The smell of cow gum characterised my office. Later coffee took its place as the defining fragrance.

Our first home was an apartment in the red light district near the station. My first car was bought from my father; it was an old Chrysler 180 with an overhead camshaft. I had the car repainted and lines added in gold to mimic a car that was racing in Formula One at the time. The only problem with the car was that it had the wrong size carburettor, which meant it did not always respond properly when you put your foot on the accelerator.

After six months at that apartment, we took the opportunity to move away from early lodgers and nocturnal slugs on the dark green patterned carpet to be closer to our newly-found church. We had discovered an Episcopal high church. This was not normally the kind of church that I would seek out, but some people there had a wonderfully frank interpretation of the faith. For example, when a storm came by and blew tiles from parishioners' houses (and this was a poor area of town), members of the congregation would get their ladders out and fix them, whether these houses belonged to churchgoers or not. Two people who particularly stood out to me were twin brothers, Peter and Paul LeFevre, who both worked as plumbers. They found a nice flat for Alison and me to move into just down the road from the church, on a steep hill called Silver Road.

A bit later on, the Edwardian vicarage of our church came on the market, as the vicar was moving into a more energy-efficient new vicarage that had been built for him, so Alison and I decided to buy the huge vicarage and turn it into the base for our band. We had a nice soundproofed music room and enough space for all the band members to have their own rooms. We did some recording down at Cambridge and a few more songs at a studio in Norwich. However, the band members wanted to go in different directions; this was partially instigated by Jerry's new wife, who was not too excited about living among the band, which is understandable. Her gerbils were let loose in the music room; clearly there was a conflict of interest.

Sadly, Magdalene broke up, but that was not the end of my musical ambitions. I started a new project called "the God-Rock Road Show". This included dancers who performed to some of the songs we played. The next project was to write a musical with the church organist, David Berwick, who worked for the stationery office as a civil servant. He used to joke that he had not moved in years. The musical was called *The Carpenter King* and was along the lines of *Godspell* and *Jesus Christ Superstar*. We decided to perform it in the church, and several of the congregation were involved. The show turned out to be a big success, with large audiences. At one point it looked as if the local theatre was going take on the show and perform it, but at the last minute they pulled out.

Following my time at the press, I applied again to the teaching college and this time was accepted. At that time, I was over-introverted and a little too self-reflective. I found that teaching drew out the best in me, forcing me to interact with the students in a positive way. It somehow helped me to be at my best. I knew that I was finally on the right track.

We eventually had to sell the vicarage, for when the band broke up some of the members moved out. They were replaced by a couple who found it impossible to pay their rent, and because of this we started to get into debt. The experience of dealing with the couple had put us off the idea of a community house. However, the best thing was that this was the house where Madeleine, our first child, was born. There is nothing more precious or wonderful in the world than the experience of adding children to your life.

Following my training, I went for an interview for a job at Great Yarmouth Grammar School. At the end of year, they announced that they had representatives from Loddon Secondary School who were looking for an English and drama teacher. I had no idea why Loddon would interview me for the position. They asked me to describe dramas I might teach. I must have done a really good job, because they offered me the position.

My degree and training had been largely in English, so when I got to the school I was quite stunned to discover that 90 percent of my teaching load would actually be drama. This was a steep learning curve for me, but one that worked out. We put on three shows when I was there, *Carpenter King, Oliver* and *Joseph*. The community loved the shows, and with great zeal some of the students got quite motivated. This was the point when I learned that music, drama, sport and art can be the elements that keep students engaged in school as they find channels to excel and to express their passion in contexts outside the classroom.

After selling the vicarage, we moved to a new four-bedroom house on a new estate. Here we became involved in the creation of a start-up ecumenical church, which was good fun and satisfied us. By this time we also had our second child, James. However Alison found the environment quite depressing and we began to feel restless. We had both grown up in Forces families, and the environment began to make us feel in need of a fresh adventure.

I applied for jobs in Australia, Canada, and Hong Kong, and was very excited to hear back from the English Schools Foundation in Hong Kong, who invited me for an interview in London. At the interview, there were two headmasters:

Jonty Driver, Head of Island School, who later went on to lead Wellington College, and Mike Taylor, who was the head of South Island School, which was, at that time, just being set up.

I must have prepared well for the interview. Jonty asked me, "What is the use of English literature?" I had memorized a quotation from Matthew Arnold who said, "Literature contains all the best in thought and in feeling." Within a few days I received a telegram offering me a job at South Island School, Hong Kong, on overseas terms. Our life was about to change radically.

We were driven down to Heathrow Airport by our local vicar with a gift of two huge suitcases from dear church friends and boarded a 747 with two small children. Alison had a perm – big curly hair. Madeleine was carrying a little red suitcase. James was clutching his Mr Man soft toy – green with a red hat.

I thought that I would feel very at home in Hong Kong because of the time I had grown up there. In fact, the whole initiation was quite a shock, from the flight and ensuing jet lag, which was an unexpected trial. We imagined that we would go to Hong Kong for two years and return to the UK. Little were we to know that this was to be a 19-year adventure, and that eventually we would spend a total of 26 years in that wonderful city.

We were met at Hong Kong airport by the legendary stench from the nullah around the airport landing strip. This was still the old airport, which extended into the sea. It was one of the most dramatic approaches in the world, as it entailed skimming over house tops in the vicinity of the runway. You could literally see into people's homes and catch sight of what was on their televisions!

The plane dropped suddenly to ensure that it had enough stopping space, as the runway terminated in the sea. "Turn left at the checkerboard" was the famous navigation instruction. The checkerboard was painted on a hillside near the harbour, and turning there meant the pilots had a good chance of successfully lining up for the runway.

Human Resources from the English Schools Foundation met us, in the form of the legendary Enid Bamforth, a formidable but gracious lady. She shepherded us onto a coach and we drove to the Merlin Hotel, an old hotel well situated in the heart of the shopping area in Tsim Sha Tsui. I felt quite disoriented but stepped out into the night to look at the main shopping road in this part of Hong Kong. The atmosphere was electrifying with the buzzing heat, the intense humidity, the traffic and the incredible illuminated signs that extended as far as the eye could see, not to mention the lights on the harbour.

The next day, we went exploring the area and found ourselves in the Ambassador Hotel arcade, which was across the road from our hotel. An Indian about 30 years old jumped out of his tailor's shop and said to me, "Excuse me, sir. This looks very funny in Hong Kong." He was pointing at my shirt sleeves – I was wearing a Marks and Spencer shirt with sleeves that were a little too short for my long arms. He said, "Come and I'll make you some shirts." I said to him, "I don't have any money on me."

"No problem, sir," he said. "As a Tai Pan, you need to dress properly." He sensed that he had the moral upper hand, and he did. By the time I left his shop, I had ordered 12 shirts. He insisted that it should be 12 shirts by quoting his mantra, 'cheaper by the dozen'. He took my address at the hotel and I walked back. The clothes were ready within 48 hours.

The name of the tailor was Danny Chandramani. Danny showed me two things about Hong Kong: How incredibly efficient the place is, and the extraordinary level of entrepreneurship. From there, we established a wonderful relationship that lasts until today.

He invited me to go to his club, which I thought sounded quite grandiose; it turned out to be the Chung King Mansions Club, which was located in one of the shabbiest and most notorious neighbourhoods in Tsim Sha Tsui. It was, in fact, a curry club. During the meal, I noticed that it was rather hot in the room, even though the air conditioner was on. Then I realised that the window was smashed; all the cold air was escaping.

Halfway through the meal, another Indian came into the small restaurant and opened the cupboard, pulled out a shirt and changed right there and then. I realised that at night this must be his bedroom.

Our next invitation was an offer to drive to the beach. Danny had recently acquired a Honda Civic. All the way to the beach and back he played me a tape of his guru, Vaswani, talking about the meaning of life in a thin, reedy voice. He was a devout follower of this guru, whom he referred to as the Divine Master, and took the religious side of his life seriously. Even though I was a Christian, I think the fact that we both felt spiritual matters were important was a foundational source of our friendship.

Years later, when I moved to Belgium, Danny called me

late at night. I could tell something was worrying him. I asked him if everything was OK and he told me that his daughter, Pooja, had passed away. I was moved that he entrusted me with his news at a time of real pain, and despite our theological differences he was quite a strong supporter.

He was a strong businessman from the Sunni caste and over the years I must have ordered about 30 suits from him, not to mention a few leather jackets. Any visit to his little shop was always accompanied by hospitality. Usually his opening line would be, “A cold beer would be nice.” Then he would pick up the phone and order some samosas, which would arrive as we were discussing fabrics for the next suit.

Hong Kong is a place where such inter-cultural friendships can flourish and where people can discover the beauty of different cultures. At heart, all people have the same issues to contend with. We have the opportunity to see very different philosophies and understandings and are able to view the meaning of life from many angles: good and evil, and what happens to us when we pass on. It requires an open mind, a love for people and patience to access the wonder of different cultures which challenge us to consider our particular views.

Danny’s advertisement read:

Our Mission is to provide Exceptional Quality Clothing at a Price Affordable to YOU!

Danny Chandiramani would like to
Thank You for your Friendship,
Loyalty, & Support!!!

Our Success would not be possible
without YOU!
The Journey of a Stylish Man
Begins here.

One of the first friends we had in Hong Kong was Tommy Tam, the civilian employee who had worked with my father back in the 1960s. He had finished his government employment and taken a retirement job involving liaison with the foreign players at the Happy Valley football club. He was still as young and sprightly, though he was more than 60 years old. His mantra was: "Health is everything. Without health you cannot do anything." He would take walks every day to keep up his fitness. When the army asked him to stay on with them for an extra couple of years, he said he would do it if they gave him his maturity service up to that point so he could invest it. He felt very disappointed when the army refused this request and he found it very hard to let the issue go from his mind, as he felt it was a sign of disrespect which went deep.

He took me one day to his house which he appropriately named Healthy Village, although it wasn't a village at all. Rather, it was a tower block in North Point, housing supplied by the government. His house was in fact one open space of about 400 square feet, which was crammed with bunk beds. This is where he had raised his family. He had a songbird that he kept on the balcony in a cage and every day, he would take the bird for a walk. This was a new concept to me, but he told me it kept the bird happy. It was a really common sight in that part of the world.

Occasionally he would ring up for a get-together and we

Early days in UK, Chris and Nick wrapped up warm

Chris on holiday with the family at Royden Court, Repulse Bay, Hong Kong

Royden Court, the scene of varied adventures

Mary, Chris, Nick and Tim enjoying Repulse Bay sunshine

Tim and Nick building on the beach

Prep School at Dunchurch, Winton Hall - check out the back row

Mary and Jim Miller beautifully dressed for a wedding

Under 14s rugby team, Lawrence Sherriff School, Rugby.
Nick the captain with best friend Richard Coss holding the ball

Second time in Hong Kong: Nick, always the sharp dresser, in our flat at Braemar Hill

Walking Lugard Road, The Peak, HK with gorgeous children Madeleine and James

Island Praise meets March for Jesus at the Waterfront TST

Nepal trek with South Island School

A day out in the beautiful islands of HK

HK: "Your dragons are in my blood"

Cley-next-the-sea, our much-loved Norfolk home and retreat

Coastal walk by Cley Mill

Nick and happy twins Katy and Peter in Kota Kinabalu

Madeleine and her beloved Dad at Tom and Jacinta's HK wedding

James and 'Mr Dad', mirroring 'cool'

PhD, Nottingham University - thanks to family and friends for their steadfast support

Leaving HK in 2000 – no one wanted to leave. Thank you David MacIntyre for the photo! Thank you rain for releasing the smiles!

Nick in a special place for many of us from Christian Centre, the Bluebell Wood, Belgium, always a springtime joy

Stranger CD, photos by David. 'Just a stranger in this world, just passing through. Got a home on high, that's where I'm sailing to'

Stranger CD, photos by David

St. John's International schooldays, a golden era in blessing and favour!

Called back to Hong Kong, to work with YHK Christian College

Nick with YMCA HK Chairman and faithful friend Mr Jack Young

Mr Tommy Tam, a lifelong friend and supporter

Nick, Tim and Chris - Mary said that due to their colouring, they were described as 'red, white and blue' when they were young.

Australian International School, Singapore. Mr Phillip Green, the High Commissioner of Australia to Singapore and Her Excellency Mrs Bernadette Cavenaugh, New Zealand High Commissioner to Singapore

Chinese New Year at AIS, the whole school gathered in the gym to welcome the New Year lucky dragon

Gatsby Gala at AIS, one of many wonderful occasions
led by AISPA Parent Association

Dressed to impress at another great AIS gathering

Portrait by Rin Watanabe, a student at AIS

Sharing the light, with birthday cupcakes. Thank you Cecilia!

The brothers meet again, Singapore in later days

Team Nick: The ever-generous Jodie Casson mobilised her lovely friends to help us. Their children were also very welcome visitors.

Plus the amazing Heidi - sunshine, encouragement and physio all in one!

The Rugby Club at AIS, a dream come true for Nick and the teams.
Cheers Jordie for all your support - you are a winner.

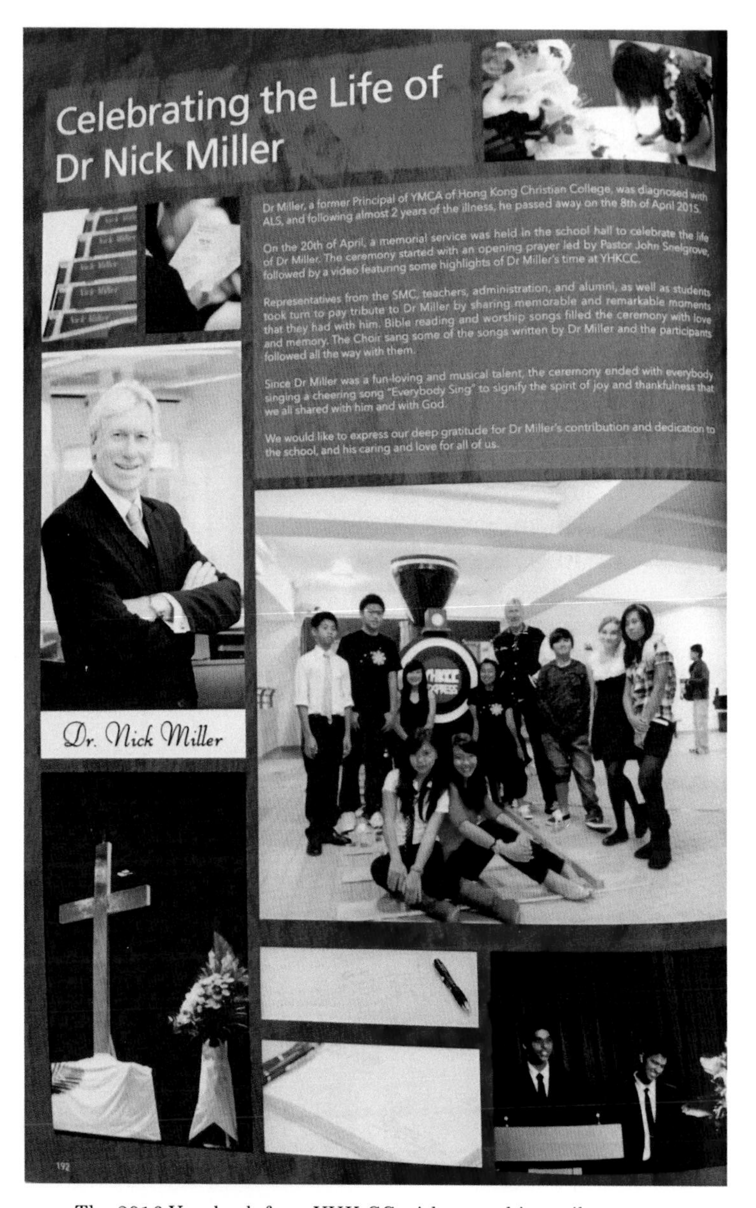

Celebrating the Life of Dr Nick Miller

Dr Miller, a former Principal of YMCA of Hong Kong Christian College, was diagnosed with ALS, and following almost 2 years of the illness, he passed away on the 8th of April 2015.

On the 20th of April, a memorial service was held in the school hall to celebrate the life of Dr Miller. The ceremony started with an opening prayer led by Pastor John Snelgrove, followed by a video featuring some highlights of Dr Miller's time at YHKCC.

Representatives from the SMC, teachers, administration, and alumni, as well as students took turn to pay tribute to Dr Miller by sharing memorable and remarkable moments that they had with him. Bible reading and worship songs filled the ceremony with love and memory. The Choir sang some of the songs written by Dr Miller and the participants followed all the way with them.

Since Dr Miller was a fun-loving and musical talent, the ceremony ended with everybody singing a cheering song "Everybody Sing" to signify the spirit of joy and thankfulness that we all shared with him and with God.

We would like to express our deep gratitude for Dr Miller's contribution and dedication to the school, and his caring and love for all of us.

The 2016 Yearbook from YHK CC with a touching tribute page.
Thank you Principal Dion Chen.

Last days in Singapore with Peter and Nick

Kate and her daddy, 2014

Church Stow, thank you Chris. An open sky, got a home on high...

Nick's painting from the 1970s The Warrior

would take him to a restaurant of his choice. At the end of the meal, he would always bring mangoes as dessert. These wonderful fruits were a family favourite and remain so. He was very proud of the fact that they were of the finest quality in the world. One day he asked me to take photos of him in his uniform, which I did.

Over time, we talked more about his disappointments in life; his son had run off, leaving him with twin girls and his wife to support. He did not feel he was respected in the family. Tommy developed a new mantra which was, "Forget, look forward and not backwards."

Later, when I moved to Belgium, I asked Candy, who was a wonderful caring lady, if she would look after Tommy for me. She became his adopted daughter. This proved to be a godsend, as one day she sent me an X-ray of Tommy's and I checked with the school nurse, who told me that the X-ray showed that Tommy had a vast cancer. I went down to Hong Kong to see him for the last time. We ended up eating a traditional Chinese meal. As we were going to the restaurant he had to keep stopping to gather his breath.

Then Candy called me in Belgium to say that Tommy had passed away. At the time when he was dying she had received a phone call that appeared to come from Tommy, though there was nobody there. They were both very special.

The accommodation took a bit of getting used to. We were in a high-rise apartment with limited space and this feeling was another thing to adjust to, especially after our place in the UK. For the first year, I missed my friends and life in the UK. This feeling gradually faded as I became addicted to the vibrancy and pace of life in Hong Kong and the dramatic sights and continual contrasts. There was the beauty of the mountains that lay behind – the elevation that allowed you to understand where you were relative to other parts of Hong Kong. The searing heat of the summer, the electric chorus of the cicadas at night, the vast purposeful movement around the city and the constant drone of the street sellers, the glamour of the high-end shops and the hotels and everywhere you went outstanding service and rapid turnover. The efficiency of the city was amazing. You would see ocean liners like the QE2 juxtaposed with the sampans with fishermen on board looking for a catch in the harbour. The Star Ferry was always making its short trip between Hong Kong and Kowloon, packed with people, plus fireboats and other boats carrying goods, all surrounded by sun reflected off the buildings.

I also liked the drama of the weather. When it rained, the force of the downpour could be more dangerous than a typhoon, washing away houses and boulders. The people would cling to umbrellas but there was no way to avoid the rain and stay dry. Alternatively, the extreme heat could catch you out if you weren't properly prepared for the beach with full sun protection. And even though it never snowed in January and February it could become very cold, with the rich breaking out their fur coats from storage, often smelling strongly of mothballs.

After a year, I was obsessed with Hong Kong; when I returned home to UK, I couldn't wait to get back to the city after our long summer break.

I mentioned that we were involved with an ecumenical church in Norwich. One day at the church a lady called Jackie Pullinger came to speak. She had written a book called *Chasing the Dragon,* which was about her involvement in helping drug addicts and triad gangsters in Hong Kong to rehabilitate through faith. I had read her book, which was pretty exciting reading, and she had a fearsome reputation. I told her that I had been interviewed for a job in Hong Kong and she took it for granted that I would be successful. She said "When you come, come and pray with us", and passed us her business card.

The vicar of the church drove us down to Heathrow airport; Alison was sporting an afro haircut. This was the 80s, 1981 to be precise. We had Madeleine and James with us. The school was in temporary accommodation in the So Kun Po area of Hong Kong, near Causeway Bay, which is one of the busiest shopping centres in Hong Kong and adjacent to Victoria Park. Stepping out into this area, you were faced with a mass of humanity with competition for space on the pavement.

The school itself was a standard government building, seven storeys high and no play facilities except one basketball court and an assembly hall. Despite the limitation of the facilities I found the school to be fantastic. The students were very responsive to teaching input and produced outstanding work. The Hong Kong work ethic rubbed off on the students, who came from high-performing families who thrived in the expat environment.

I was the home-room teacher for a secondary year 4 class, a number of whom are still in touch with me to this day. They have nourished me with some wonderful statements about how I made a difference in their lives and inspired them with a love for literature. I don't remember how I did that, but making a difference in children's lives is the aspiration of every teacher, hence very gratifying. Those statements were very precious and I treasure them.

I was 27 years old and it seemed that since I had entered the teaching profession life had got better and better. I had a clear direction to go in and a moral purpose for my life. Each day was an adventure. The teachers were unlike any I had met before. They had incredible confidence and stature, and the leaders of the major departments shared their thoughts with conviction and insight. They exuded the sense that we were a high-performing school and that it was a privilege to be associated with it.

We had a few teachers who had been drafted from Island School, which was the ESF's first secondary school and had already established an excellent reputation. This way they exported a successful school culture to the new South Island School. At first I had been a little disappointed that I wasn't going to work for Jonty Driver, because our connection had been so positive at the interview. However, within a short time I began to appreciate Mike Taylor more and more. He was a very principled person and a committed Quaker. When the Falklands war broke out, he described it as a tragedy, which of course a war is. He had a great blend of humanity with a clear vision and direction for the school. Plus he was consultative, which made the staff feel they were being treated with respect.

I had a position where I was learning important skills that would benefit me in later life, and I immediately got involved in extra-curricular activities. I coached the basketball team and started a Friday night youth club with the music teacher, John Meir, who now lives in Australia. I introduced a form of indoor rugby in the assembly hall. Basically this was a game without rules, except when a try was scored. The students absolutely loved it. After a few weeks I decided to cancel it as the kids were getting a bit too crazy. The youth club was a huge success. It really was great to see the students so happy.

At the same time I was involved with John in rewriting parts of the *Carpenter King* musical, adding new songs and dialogue. We set up auditions and soon had assembled an enthusiastic cast. The show was a very big success. They made a TV programme to be aired locally about the musical, and there is a Facebook page dedicated to it even now. The government asked us if we would be interested in putting on the show at City Hall. I consulted with the students but they were feeling quite exhausted after the run of shows and we decided against taking up the offer. This, in some ways, I regret.

Soon after *Carpenter King*, Mike Taylor announced that it was time to resign as the Head and look for a regular teaching job back in the UK. I felt hugely disappointed, as I have discovered good head teachers are hard to find. In fact in my whole career I have only worked with one other head teacher who I felt had a great blend of qualities and gained the respect of both staff and students.

The reason Mike put forward his resignation was that he felt as the head teacher that he was always running. He wanted to slow down the pace. The ESF were looking for a new Head of Island school at the same time. We had the chance to meet the two final candidates, one of whom was Colin Niven, who went on to be the head of Alleyns School and was a pioneer in setting up high quality schools in China. He was later awarded the OBE. Our new Head was a classics scholar from Cambridge; however, he found it hard to make an impact on the school as it was now well set up, well-structured and with powerful middle management.

Within two years of arriving at the school, I was promoted to Head of English. This was one of the jobs that I have enjoyed the most in my career. We had a team of fine, creative and well-motivated teachers who were committed to improvement. We enjoyed each other's company and met regularly to share ideas and distribute administrative functions.

Another year later I was promoted to the role of Senior Teacher and took responsibility for the assemblies, which helped me gain confidence in front of large groups of students. One more year later, I was selected to be Deputy Principal, with responsibility for the school's pastoral care. By now we had moved into our new permanent building, which was situated on the south side of Hong Kong island and surrounded by lush vegetation.

One of the most inspirational teachers was the art teacher, Brian Tilbrook. He had flowing white hair and he was always on the lookout for areas of the school that he could improve. His improvements usually entailed the use of either gold spray - for example, he sprayed trees or interesting driftwood that he had found along the beach - or the introduction of water features. In many murky spots of the school we would hear the sound of water trickling from a fountain he had created. One such water feature was installed in the foyer of the school. Hundreds of people passed it every day, and it pleased parents and visitors to the school.

One day I arrived at the school around 7.30 am only to find Brian's water feature in the lobby surrounded by policemen. I asked what was going on. The office manager said a cobra had taken up residence in the fountain area and apparently had been there for some time. Fortunately the snake was captured and relocated a long way from the school, or so I was told. I wouldn't be surprised if the snake didn't make it back to the hills, as snake is a speciality in Chinese cuisine.

Since retiring, Brian has continued to produce art of his own with major exhibitions in various parts of the world. He's a man who's a great example to children that many achievements can be made throughout their lives. I am the proud possessor of some of his artworks. A major piece hangs between the Conrad and the Shangri-La hotels and other pieces can be seen in many of the Cathay offices around the world. He was also asked by the HK government to commission a series of stamps commemorating heritage sites in the territory.

Brian's encounters with water were not limited to fountains. At his farewell speech he expressed his frustration with the taps in the male toilets, which were a style of tap which released water for a limited time when pressed down. However, the water came out at such a high pressure that it would soak the unwary user. This led in turn to many ribald jokes about Brian being incontinent. His final gift to the school was a new set of taps in the male toilet so that others would not be the butt of similar jokes. The way he expressed it was that when you had been to the toilet the tap would pee back at you.

This is not the only story about the male toilets. I was passing them one day when a teacher called Tommy Smith ran out of the door in a panic. His face was completely white. I asked what the matter was. He said that he had been sitting on the toilet nearest the open window, which opened onto the jungle outside, and as he reached for the toilet paper that was recessed into the wall, a giant tree frog had jumped at him, which scared him so much that he left at high speed. He became the teacher who had come closest to wiping his backside with a frog.

Around 1985, I was intrigued by the mystical country of Tibet. That was the year our twins were born. I had a friend called Julian Hawken, who was an intrepid Kiwi. He had had consumed too much LSD in earlier years and finally had a life-changing experience with God which helped him change his ways for the better. As a professional photographer, he had a desire to visit Tibet. He wanted to take pictures and literature to Lhasa city. He asked me if I would like to go with him. Alison graciously supported the trip, and we went with cameras and literature in hand. We set off with only a rough idea how we would get to Lhasa. We were lucky to get special passes to go there, as it was a closed city at that time. The first part of the trip was via train to Xing via Xian, where we were privileged to see the terracotta warriors. I picked up messages which I still have.

After that we found that we would need to continue via bus. We decided that we had better eat something before the bus left, so we found a restaurant and pointed at a few raw ingredients. The cook was an old lady who put together a noodle dish with fried egg on the top. We then boarded the bus for the 36-hour trip to Lhasa. Julian and I were seated over the rear wheel, which was extremely uncomfortable. The bus was leaking diesel from somewhere and the smell invaded the cabin. Worst of all the bus was filthy, the seats were too small and all the way to Lhasa I tasted nothing but egg. I did not eat an egg for years afterwards!

We finally arrived at the Snowlands Hotel, where a lady would always wink at us with freshly made yoghurt she brought to sell. At the hotel I discovered that she didn't have any teeth.

Whilst in Tibet and particularly in Lhasa, I visited a number of bars in some fascinating places with Julian. People, and Buddhist priests in particular, were very friendly and interested in Julian's religion. One of the barmen asked him for a copy of the Bible, which was not generally available in that country. We also visited the majestic Potala palace. When we walked in, there didn't seem to be anyone around, so we took ourselves on a self-guided tour. Wonderful.

Julian decided that he wanted to return home via Kathmandu. I was feeling that I had already been away too long. We visited the local telephone exchange, which despite the antiquated equipment somehow connected me with Alison back in Hong Kong. I asked her whether she thought I should go with Julian to Kathmandu. In a remarkably restrained voice she said "I think it's time you came home now". There was a snowstorm at the time.

I managed to get a flight from Lhasa direct to HK, which was unusual. I was seated next to a soldier from the Red Army who it seemed had never flown before. He was terrified, gripping the armrest with intensity. The stewardess offered to sell me a gift, a ceramic horse. I didn't know how much these gifts added to the fuel bill. My departure was fortuitous for Julian, as it allowed him to continue a romantic liaison with Monica, a wonderful Swedish lady who later became his wife.

Insanely, it also prevented him acquiring a criminal record. This honour went to me.

Julian decided to visit an extremely auspicious monastery after I had gone. He told me that there was very clearly a sign on the door saying that photography was prohibited. In Julian's case, this was a like red rag to a bull, and he went inside and started taking pictures. A number of the monastery staff came and told him to stop. He ignored the instruction but failed to notice that the monastery had become extremely quiet and that the front door had been locked. The next thing that happened was a police van arrived. They asked Julian to accompany them, and Julian resisted arrest. Finally they bundled him into the police van and took him to the police station, where they asked him to show them the pass we had been given to allow us to visit Lhasa. There were two names on the paper, mine and his. They asked him what his name was. He pointed to my name, and as a result I now have a criminal record in Tibet.

Whenever Julian tells the story, he laughs so hard that tears roll down his face. I am still trying to figure out a way to get even with him. Needless to say Julian and I are still firm friends, together with his wife and two children.

The experience of being at such high altitude and seeing the streams of opaque water cascading down the mountain inspired this poem.

Awaken

Upon a mountain top amid untried Tibetan peaks,

Then the slumbering glaciers will groan back to wakefulness

From beneath their blankets of numbing cold,

And rouse to score your name on sides of granite
As their steely aloofness slowly descends into rivers of melting love
I will stand and shout my love for you.
Rivers which spray from their opaque wintry source
In cascading rapids and waterfalls,
As white torrents of burning-cold passion,
Racing with ecstatic hope.
Gradually their way broadens majestically
Approaching the palace where you recline
Among amber-coloured petals in Indian climes
Sighing for fulfilment of half-remembered dreams
As damask curtains wave in the soft balmy breeze,
Lifting their tones expectantly at the quickening of your heart.
The heavy blossoms take wing, fluttering on the moist winds,
Casting their final offering of narcotic perfume
From the carpeted ground which serves as the path
For our souls to meet across untended borders of time and space.
Cast away those empty sighs and restless dreams,
And insects' electric murmurings harmonise
For speeded by the sorrows of loneliness,
Lifted by the prayers of the faithful,
Guided by the songs of the spirit,
Upon this fragrant way, I come to you.

Back in Hong Kong, the leaders of the church thought it would be good to have a church outing to the beach, so we loaded up two buses with children and headed for South Bay, which is near the famous Repulse Bay. However, on the way the drivers said that we could not go to South Bay because they did not have space to turn around there. Instead they recommended Middle Bay. We duly complied and got off the buses, which then drove off. Gradually we noticed that there was something unusual about the clientele. There were no children on the beach and no ladies either; in fact, the beach was totally populated by male couples, some of them engaged in displays of affection for each other. It was not long before the children noticed the unusual demographic and the rest of the afternoon was taken up trying to explain the sociological phenomenon to the children. After an uncomfortable two hours we were relieved to see the buses return. We headed for the nearest McDonalds to restore our equilibrium.

Back at school, things were not going well with our new headmaster. His behaviour started to become erratic. For example, we were never sure whether he would turn up for assemblies or not, so I had to step in for him if he didn't show up. He was also rather cynical about school improvement and education developments such as teacher appraisals. His view was that educational developments were just circular, with ideas coming into fashion then out again.

Rumours started to circulate about him. Students reported that they had seen him in the supermarket with his trolley full of vodka bottles and other alcohol. We noticed that he kept a fruit juice on his desk, and one day I noticed a drink bottle hidden in his opened drawer. He would cover up the vodka with the fruit juice. One day his secretary came to me in a fluster, saying the CEO was coming over to the school and the head was out cold on the carpet in his office. I rushed over to his office, woke him and told him that the CEO was on the way, just in time to avoid him being discovered.

This situation went on for a number of years, until one day the Chief Education Officer said to me, "I know about the Head's problem". I felt a great sense of relief, until I heard his follow-up statement. He said "If he ever gets too bad, give me a call and I'll come over and take him home". Eventually I found the stress of the situation too difficult and decided to look for another job.

The Chairman of the Board paid me a visit. He said to me, "Nick, we know you've been running the school and we know you're applying for other jobs, but we want to say that we see you as the next Head of this school, and we want you to stop applying for other jobs". By this time I had gained a sense of responsibility for the school; staff tended to refer to me for decisions rather than the Head, and I felt a huge sense of commitment to the place. It had become almost like a family to me. Therefore, the Chairman's words meant a lot and I believed them.

Within a relatively short time the Head had resigned and his post was advertised. Naturally I applied. There had been a new Chief Education Officer appointed. I sat in my office waiting for the decision to be announced. Three people arrived at my door: the new CEO, the Chairman and Deputy Chairman of the Board. They announced to me that they had decided to appoint a candidate from outside, from the UK.

I was devastated, as I felt I had been lied to. I had felt so devoted to the school during some difficult years. A promise had been broken. When the announcement of the new appointment was made to the staff, there was a resounding silence; you could have heard a pin drop. The decision was not popular with the staff.

This kind of disappointment happens to people in all

professions on a daily basis, but there is something about the community nature of a school that makes such happenings all the more personal, and I went through a grieving process for quite a while. However, this was the emotional fuel that I ultimately turned to good, as it fired my determination to undertake and ultimately complete my PhD, which acted as a kind of catharsis.

CHAPTER FIVE

ADVENTURES IN MUSIC AND EDUCATION

One thing I learned from my experience at South Island School is that God sometimes closes doors as well as opening them. It's part of our maturing walk with the Lord to learn to trust Him when the door is closed, even when it is something we really want to happen. He has wisdom far beyond ours. At the same time He loves us and is true to us. When He closes a door it is for our benefit. The best thing we can do is tell Him that we trust Him despite our feelings of disappointment. It may well have been that my connection with the staff was too close to enable me to be effective to make the hard decisions that all leadership entails from time to time.

I began the study project as an M Phil, as I had already done enough questionnaires related to the work I had been undertaking. I had been introducing an appraisal system at South Island School which had a strong focus on teacher development. The ESF professional development centre at the Sarah Roe Centre suggested that I should contact Nottingham University, with whom they had established links. They accepted me to do my M. Phil and assigned me to work with Professor Chris Day. After a couple of years of working on the thesis part time, he organised an upgrading committee and my study was upgraded to PhD status. The terms of the upgrade included my spending a number of weeks per year at the university, which I did during the Easter and summer holidays.

Chris Day was a great help and inspiration in the study. His own Christian faith was a further point of connection. Candy Leung, who was my secretary at the time, undertook the typing, and the rate of turnover of my manuscript made sure that I got the project moving forward. Ultimately the PhD took about five years to complete and was awarded in 1997. The viva was conducted by Professor John Eliot, whose writing I respected a great deal. I think the thesis enabled me to understand the context I had been working in more completely and enabled me to transcend the sense of betrayal I had been feeling.

At this time I also met Professor David Hopkins, and there was talk of my joining the university as a lecturer. However I felt my calling was to schools rather than academia, and declined the invitation. I shall always be grateful to Nottingham University, and Chris Day in particular, for helping me to move to another level in my understanding of schools from a theoretical point of view. This understanding has served me well in succeeding years. The main topics of the study were institutional culture, leadership and change management.

When we moved to Hong Kong we started to attend St John's Cathedral, which my family had also attended when I was a child. This haven of peace in the middle of Central has a special atmosphere of calm and refreshment. During our time there, I spent a few years helping with the youth ministry. However the catalyst for deeper fellowship was a visit from Marilyn Baker, a blind piano player and worship leader. The organisers of her visit to Hong Kong were looking for musicians to support her at her meetings. We got on extremely well and in the wake of her visit, a new praise and worship ministry was born, called Island Praise.

This involved a number of people who have become lifelong friends, including Stephen and Hilary Russell-Smith of the NatWest Bank, John and Sandra Snelgrove, employed by AXA insurance, Paul and Vicky Savage, who worked for Cable and Wireless, Laing and Yvonne Fleming of China Light and Power and Tim and Alison, who were with the British Army. Tony and Drusilla Read were also part of this founding group. Tony worked with a major construction company.

What we lacked in musical prowess we made up for in enthusiasm. This was at a point when contemporary praise and worship was still in its infancy in Hong Kong and we found ourselves invited to all kinds of places to lead worship, including a prison in Macau, a Vietnamese refugee camp and churches which included St John's Cathedral, Ambassador Church, Union Church, the Lighthouse Church, St Andrew's Church and others.

This was when I met Jym Kay, the drummer with Citybeat. Jym had a contract with Polygram records. The unusual thing about them was that their lead singer, John Laudon, who was Canadian, performed the lead vocals in Cantonese.

Jym and I established a very strong bond of friendship that has endured over the years. Our musical tastes were pretty similar, and he had a strong passion for outreach. When the Connaught Road, Central was closed during public holidays he would often obtain a permit for us to set up our PA and play in front of the HSBC.

Ultimately we produced a CD, mostly of songs that I had written. We produced about 3000 CDs and managed to sell them all. This was a very exciting moment for us. This was the first time I was asked to sign my autograph on a record. I have a photo to prove how surprised I was!

We were to hear the album being played in all kinds of odd places. For example, some friends reported that it had been played on a tour bus that was taking them to the Great Wall of China. Others heard it in an Indian curry house. Another story attached to the Island Praise record involved an American military officer. He was attending the same church as us and had acquired a copy of the record, which he enjoyed a lot. He had memorised a number of the songs. When he was on a trip to China with another military officer, at a time when relations between the US and China were strained, he was arrested by the Chinese authorities along with his colleague. They were accused of spying. For a number of days his fate was unclear. There was intense diplomatic dialogue between the US and China about the officers and they were finally released after about a week in jail. The next time I saw him at church he told me that during this period of uncertainty, the songs from the record had encouraged him. He said he wanted to do something for me by way of a thank you, and suggested that next time the US 7th Fleet were in town, he would arrange for me to have a visit to a US naval vessel. He kept his word and the ship that we toured was the aircraft carrier the USS *Carl Vincent*. This ship was amazing, with over 3000 personnel on board. What impressed me the most was the opportunity to get close to F16 aircraft on the flight deck. It brought to life the movie *Top Gun*, which has always been a favourite of mine because of the flight sequences.

The Island Praise era was an exciting and rewarding time, culminating in the biggest audience we had ever played for, at the beginning of the first Hong Kong March for Jesus. We played for about 15,000 people in the HK Coliseum.

Early on in Hong Kong, I dug out the card that Jackie Pullinger had given to me in the UK and called her up. She invited me over to their St Stephen's Society apartment in Babington Path, Mid Levels. She was a lady with tremendous drive, immense leadership ability and true vision.

We used to enjoy the fellowship times with the Brothers, as she called them. These were mostly ex-drug addicts and triads. There was a little bit of a lull in her ministry at this point and she found time to come over to our apartment, enjoying such things as blowing up balloons for Madeleine's seventh birthday party. Being a clarinet player helped! She also took me and Madeleine to view the Walled City, which was still standing at that time. A rabbit warren of grey corridors and open sewers, it had a reputation for lawless behaviour. This is where she had established her ministry, which can be read about in her book *Chasing the Dragon.*

Soon afterwards, she was given some premises by the government, called Hang Fook Camp in Cheung Sha Wan and the scale of her ministry grew rapidly. Currently she has a new permanent site at Shatin. Jackie is a courageous lady and a true champion of the Gospel. Her ministry has changed, and saved, numerous lives. I can illustrate this through an example from my own school. There was a student who had just completed his GCSEs and had only managed to pass four, with poor grades. I heard on the grapevine that he was involved with drugs, specifically heroin. His mother requested that we accept him to do A levels, but I made the decision not to re-admit him to the sixth form, on academic and social grounds. His mother was of course very upset with my decision.

The next thing that happened was that I was summoned to the nurses' station in school. The boy's sister was in the sick bay, but she would not tell the nurse what the problem was. I questioned the girl who had accompanied her. I began to get a very bad feeling about the situation and made the decision to take the girl to a hospital. With her friend, a school prefect, accompanying her, I carried her to my car and drove to the Adventist Hospital, the nearest hospital to the school. On the way to the hospital the girl admitted to me that she had overdosed on Panadol. To be exact, she had taken 90 tablets. I took her straight to emergency and the doctor attended to her immediately. I had asked the school to call her parents about the situation. The doctor told me that there was no more that I could do and I took the prefect to stay with the girl until the father arrived.

I needed to get back to school because I was concerned about the leadership situation and was aware that I had a responsibility back at the school to make sure all was running smoothly. As I was climbing out of the hospital I saw the father arrive by taxi. I expected the parents to thank me for taking action that had possibly saved the girl's life. However, because of the situation with the son, they chose to attack me for not remaining at the hospital to meet the parents face to face. Of course I felt disappointed by this, but it was another lesson in the politics of the school.

Things with the son went from bad to worse. He had dreams of being a rock star and was involved with a band in which he played bass. His addiction grew stronger and his regard for his own life grew weaker. Behind all this, the parents were experiencing difficulties at home in their marriage. The son decided to try mixing the heroin with toilet water and injecting himself. As a result, he contracted hepatitis and finished up in hospital. He was subsequently connected with Jackie Pullinger and became part of her rehab programme, which actually saved his life.

Later, he moved back to the UK, and I received an email from him a couple of years later. He had married a Taiwanese girl and asked me to write a reference for him as part of a university application. Even though he had not finished his A levels I knew that his life had changed completely and that as with all kids, he had immense potential. I wrote a very supportive reference for him and I'm glad to say he was accepted for a Bachelors course in Social Studies. The story got better from there. He was accepted to do a Master's degree at Oxford. Later, he returned to Hong Kong, and to bring it all full circle he became the careers teacher at a school where I had been Headmaster. Currently he is studying for his PhD at Hong Kong University.

Another memorable young person from that era was Carlos, who was part of Jackie's rehab group and had also been involved with serious drugs. Carlos told me recently that my interest in Christian music had inspired him to get involved in worship leading. Carlos is half-Filpino and half-Korean. To me he has an outstanding voice and is incredibly musically gifted.

Our connection, dating from his time in rehab, ended with him singing on three of the five albums that it's been my privilege to record up to this point. I'm glad to say that Carlos is now healthy and well, and happily married with two children. Following time spent as a pastor in the Philippines, he has now reconnected with Jackie's ministry in Hong Kong. Such is his dedication to Jackie that he turned down an opportunity to serve as a worship leader with a major Christian ministry in the United States.

These episodes taught me two things. First, there are a lot of kids with problems which find their root in difficulties at home, particularly in relation to their parents. Secondly, it helped to develop a belief that every student can achieve something worthwhile, and especially in relation to the talents which every student has. It is an important responsibility of the school to help students find what their gifts and talents are and to develop their potential in relation to them.

We must instil within each student that we believe in them and that they should not compare themselves to others, because each person has a unique set of gifts and there is an important role for every child to play in their lives. Adolescents in particular experience a lot of self-doubt when they are students. We must let them know that they matter, we must support them emotionally and we must give them hope and vision. We must let them know that they are uniquely talented and that their lives matter.

The ESF knew of my work in teacher appraisal and developed through a working party an appraisal system which they wanted introduced across their 15 schools. They asked me if I would take the role of leading the training of the 400 teachers they employed at that time. I asked for volunteers from across the schools and was pleasantly surprised by the positive response. We soon had a team of 30 trainers. Over a two-year period we introduced teacher appraisal across all the schools, which involved goal setting and classroom observation. The team was delightful to work with. We were professional, hard-working, inspiring, collaborative and fun. The events went very well and feedback from the teachers was very positive.

When I was one year into this role, the ESF asked me if I would like to lead their for-profit arm, which had been established on paper but was not truly operational. As part of my PhD study I had read a lot of business literature, particularly in relation to leadership and change. The idea of business seemed fascinating to me, and this was a great opportunity that I had been given.

I subsequently became the first General Manager of ESF Educational Services Limited. The company had a very small start-up budget, but ESF had a great name in the educational community in Hong Kong. For my first project

I set up English as a Second Language (ESL) camps during the summer holidays, using ESF schools as the venues. I asked for payment with application, so we had a lot of money upfront. With this I was able to hire the teachers we needed. The enrolment was extremely strong and the company grew exponentially. We added on a sports section, which was also very popular. We also offered a number of in-service training events to other schools and developed educational psychology services. This leadership experience was invaluable. It taught me about motivating staff, the importance of vision and of teamwork.

After my third year of running the company, I became a little unsure about aspects of the relationship between a big company and its parent organisation. Nevertheless, I had learned an immense amount about how to lead a successful enterprise, and this again would stand me in good stead in my teaching career.

Schools I believe are first and foremost communities, but they are complex places and undoubtedly the financial dimension is extremely important. The school must self-sustain, but also have resources to develop and upgrade infrastructure. Because of my reservations, I asked to go back into the school administration, as ultimately this was where I felt my calling to be.

I was then invited to be Deputy Head of West Island School under a new Head called Brian Driver. He was in my opinion an excellent principal, and I learned a lot from him about when to seek consensus and when to take unilateral decisions with full explanations to the stakeholders.

Human nature always gravitates towards comfort, and the problem sometimes with consensus is that the decision can be based on what is most comfortable for the teacher rather than what is in the best interests of the parents or students. A good head needs to set out a very clear vision and plan, and then have enough courage to realise the plan. At the same time, he must be sensitive enough to know when the staff have reached saturation point in the process. Otherwise, resistance and sabotage set in.

Brian‘s experience of headship served to show me a new approach from which I could learn. I think it is essential for anyone seeking leadership positions to work with one or two people who really know what they are doing and are successful in their field, as Brian undoubtedly was.

When I look back on my last three headships, the person who has taken over from me in each case has been my deputy. The strength of this is that the direction of the school and the operational structures can remain unchanged if they are working well, which means a minimum of disruption to a successfully operating school. Appointing an *in situ* deputy means you have appointed someone who understands why things are the way they are and the reasons behind particular decisions. I believe it is part of the responsibility of a Head to mentor the next generation of leaders and provide a role model for them.

The West Island School building was very new and constructed with an interesting design. My office had the misfortune to overlook an immense graveyard, so I enjoyed moving around the school and visiting classrooms rather than contemplating our ultimate demise. It was rumoured that the government offered the West Island site to the ESF because of the poor "feng shui" resulting from its proximity to the graveyard.

I am a huge believer in visiting classrooms, and find that generally both teachers and students welcome this. It is also a great way of keeping yourself informed about the quality of the teaching and learning that is going on. This connects with the business philosophy of 'management by walking about' - MBWA. Every school has a lot of policies and generally the management have little idea as to whether these policies are being enacted in the classroom. Visiting classrooms is the only way to find out.

One more important happening during our time in Hong Kong took place at the Matilda Hospital upon the Peak. Alison was pregnant. I had a funny feeling that it could be twins and I asked her whether she had twins in her family. I knew I did not have any in mine. She said "No, of course not". However, when we went for the three-month scan, the doctor said to Alison "I think your husband had better see this". I was called in to a darkened room where there was a TV monitor. The doctor pointed at the screen and said "There is one heart beating, and there is the other. Congratulations, you have twins on the way!"

This was a somewhat overwhelming thought. Both Alison and I came from families of three siblings. The idea of two at once sounded like quite a challenge. However, one of the great things about Hong Kong was that you could hire domestic help very cheaply.

When we brought the twins home from the hospital they were both sharing the same basket. We decided to call in at our favourite Chinese restaurant, the Sweet Garden (our family called it the Sweet Pea in honour of Popeye) near our apartment. The waiter nearly dropped her tray when she looked in the basket. I'm pretty sure she thought we had a two-headed baby!

Besides our twins, the children of my brother Tim, who was working at the same school, were also born at the Matilda. When his daughter Claire was born, I wrote this poem.

Claire de lune

In the hospital
There's a cry that pierces the air in a room
The captains of the commercial vessels
High over the western approaches
Are not aware
A baby has been born
Christmas is two months away
Near their fires in the hills of Palestine
The shepherds don't yet know
Nor do they dream that the birth of a child
Could bring light or warmth to their night watch
Choirs of angels announced Christ's birth to a cold
Sleeping world that might have dreamed on oblivious
This poem is my welcome to that new life in room 301A
May your star sing like angels heralding
Hope in this twilight world.

23.10.1990

We had a spacious apartment on the 14th floor with good views towards Kowloon and particularly overlooking the airport runway from Hong Kong side. Though the height of the apartment had many advantages in terms of view, it also had a couple of disadvantages. I gave a Fisher Price tape recorder to my son for Christmas, stamped "Unbreakable." This became a challenge for him. He threw it out of the bedroom window to see if it would live up to the advertising. Unfortunately, it exploded into a million pieces.

I had a rock band at the time which we called Raw Silk. I remember coming back late one night from a gig at HMS *Tamar*, which was a shore-based training and administration centre. As I got to the lobby of our building, I saw a familiar little brown furry object on the ground. I recognized it; it was the body of our pet hamster. The cage had been left open during cleaning and the animal had fallen from our utility room on the 14th floor of our building. It was a very sad moment.

The hamster was not the only casualty associated with my rock and roll exploits. There is an interesting scar on my leg, running from under the kneecap quite a long way down towards my ankle. We had just finished setting up our gear to play at the HK Fringe Club. Suddenly all the lights went out and we were plunged into darkness. The way off the stage was by means of box steps abutting the stage. These were movable, and somebody had moved them about two feet forward, away from the front of the stage.

I stepped into the darkness, expecting the steps to be in their correct position. Instead I stepped into thin air, catching my shin on the back of the box step. Again blood flowed. It was too close to the beginning of the concert to get medical help, so I played the show, which was a combination of classic rock and original songs with Ozzie Osborne-like visual effects and occasional screams and yells, inspired more by pain than by rock and roll passion. I went to the hospital after the show, where they gave me twelve stitches and sent me home.

One morning after playing at a late night show for TV with my new band, Lion Rock, a video which I believe is even now available on YouTube, I was hoping for a lie-in. This was not to be. The twins came running into our bedroom and said there was an aeroplane in the sea. We said, 'Oh it's probably just the angle you are looking at it'. They said no, it was in the sea. So we got up and saw that they were right. It was an Air China Boeing 747 that had run off the end of the runway and gone into the sea. There was no loss of life, but the plane was a write-off.

A few days later we were all woken by an explosion about 6 am. They had decided to dynamite the tail of the airplane so that things would be safer for other planes taking off or landing.

I recall one more plane accident, in bad weather when a Trident aircraft was taxiing back to the terminal to disembark. The pilot lost his bearings and drove the aircraft off the runway and into the sea. A number of cabin crew were drowned. The new airport at Chep Lap Kok is much safer and has much more space, with no serious mishaps to date.

Coming back to Raw Silk, we enjoyed playing classic rock and probably the highlight of our career was an invitation to play on TV. I'm not sure whether my students were impressed or amused, but it was a great experience, which I repeated with the next band, the above-mentioned Lion Rock. This was led by Jym Kay who had been the drummer in City Beat and was one of my closest personal friends. Our performance can still be viewed on YouTube.

Jym seemed to have bad luck with animals. He bought a small dog which he called Minnie. The dog was not very well behaved. One time when I called him at home, our conversation was continually interrupted by Jym correcting the dog: 'Minnie, get down from there! Minnie, you can't be on the cushion! Minnie, stop gnawing my drumsticks! Minnie... oh no, she's just eaten my lunch!" However, one day our conversation seemed remarkably uninterrupted by reference to Minnie, until suddenly the line went dead. I subsequently found out that during our conversation, Minnie had been gnawing her way through the phone line. That was the last straw - Minnie was advertised in the paper. The prospective purchaser asked if Jym could meet him at the exit turnstile of the local Mongkok MTR Station. The purchaser did not want to bear the cost of exiting the station and then re-entering, which would have meant paying for an extra journey. This was typical Hong Kong style. The purchaser took one look at the dog over the railings, handed over the agreed purchase price to Jym and then disappeared down to the bowels of the MTR.

Jym however found life a bit too tame after Minnie left. He purchased two budgies, which he christened Flipper and Lassie. When he went on holiday he asked me to look after them for him, which I duly agreed to do. We found the budgies were noisy, so we put them in the utility area, near the washing machine. This seemed to keep them very excited and entertained. Strangely when Jym got back from holiday, he was reluctant to retrieve his budgies. We held onto them for him for several weeks, but eventually during one of his visits to our apartment, we presented him with the cage containing Lassie and Flipper. He did not seem at all pleased to be reunited with his pets.

The next day there was a knock on our door and Jym was standing on the doormat. He had with him the cage containing his budgies. "You've got to take these back man, couldn't sleep at all last night," he said. "These things are so noisy." I didn't have the heart to turn him down.

The initial pair were soon joined by other budgie refugees from families who seemed to equate our ability to raise four kids with limitless capacity for raising budgies. Jym gave us a supply of bird seed. We topped up their feeding tray on a daily basis. These budgies seemed to have the secret of eternal life. We kept them for years and years, yet they showed no sign of moving on to Budgie Heaven. I began to wonder if I should start to supplement my diet with the budgie bird seed, on the theory that this would extend my life by some considerable margin. Jym's response? "Those China budgies, they live forever."

Following this, Jym was officially petless. However, he found that the local wildlife was inexplicably drawn to him and his apartment in Mongkok. He started to be visited by rats. He bought sticky rat traps, and when the rats were stuck on the board he would put them in a black bin bag and dispose of them outside in the public garbage bins.

Jym is one of the most authentic and dedicated missionaries I have ever met. It seems that everything he begins prospers. He began a citywide youth ministry called Saturday Night Alive (SNA), which featured contemporary worship with leaders such as Carlos and multi-media presentations. He led a fellowship of about 200 young people who went on outreach missions to the Philippines and Thailand.

Around that time I was invited to join a church called Repulse Bay Baptist Church by the newly-appointed pastor.

He came from a Pentecostal background, which may not seem the obvious pick for a Baptist church. I agreed to move because the pastor was a friend and needed support in his new situation. We agreed to move from the Cathedral, after 10 years there, to his church to be a support to him.

Jym wanted SNA to come under the accountability of the church, and I said I would talk to the pastor of the Repulse Bay Baptist Church to see if this was a possibility. Soon everything was agreed and SNA became the youth outreach ministry of RBBC. When we had been at the church for a short while, we began to see why the pastor felt he needed support. The congregation did not seem to appreciate his preaching and began to vote with their feet. The church congregation started to decline from 400 down to around 50.

During this period, I was asked to join the eldership team. I asked some of the existing elders what they thought about me joining. They said that since I was now involved in the worship, it would seem a natural fit. What they didn't tell me was that they were planning to resign. When I joined the eldership, I was surprised that there were only three other remaining members of the once sizable team.

As time went on, the financial picture became increasingly worrying as people left the church. This led to rows between the pastor and the treasurer. By the time the congregation reached 50 we had an operating budget that sustained the church for only two months. The Treasurer resigned and one of the remaining elders left for a seminary in the USA. This left just two elders: myself and a man of outstanding faithfulness, Tony Read.

Things looked increasingly desperate, and with just one

month's operating budget left, I decided that I needed to talk to the pastor. Simply put, we could not afford to continue to pay him. I met him for lunch at the YMCA, and tried to explain how serious the predicament was. He suggested that I should resign from the eldership. This was not possible, because the church was set up as a company with the elders as directors and the law required two directors for a company. If I resigned, the church would cease to function as a legal entity. HK law required two directors who were elders, and Tony and I were the remaining elders.

I said the only solution I could see was for him to resign as pastor. He agreed within a short period of time and concentrated his efforts on teaching English as a Foreign Language at one of the major banks. We tried to be generous in severance - he was given three months' salary, all the furniture in his apartment and the car that had been supplied by the church. Most of the remaining members of the church were hardcore supporters of the pastor and saw his resignation as the work of myself and Tony. However the choice came down to either the pastor leaving or the church becoming insolvent and having to shut up shop.

We had a huge amount of youth work, which in contrast to the church, was doing very well. I did not want the church to disappear because of this. I checked with Tony and we appointed four new elders to the church leadership. Within a short period we had changed its name to the Vine Christian Fellowship and moved its location to the Regal Hotel in the Causeway Bay area.

Initially we decided that we would run the new church with the eldership group taking turns to do the preaching. I, for the most part, led the worship. We steadily became more stable and financially solid, even though numbers attending the services were not great. Within a year, one of the elders resigned due to family circumstances and John Snelgrove, one of my close friends, became the replacement elder on a team of 6.

I was very happy that we had kept the church alive, albeit in a new incarnation. The youth ministry continued to thrive under Jym Kay and the elders met each Saturday for breakfast. We were a coherent and positive team, united in our desire to see the Vine Church succeed.

At first, it was quite hard going. There were big demands on the leaders who needed to cover many areas such as finance, preaching, children's ministry and worship ministry. But over time, things began to stabilize and the congregation began to grow. After five years, I felt that the church was in a stable place and that it was time for me to look again at career possibilities that might take me out of Hong Kong. After I left, Tony and John became church pastors and did a fantastic job of overseeing the growth of the church. Initially they moved the church to Central, which would make it more accessible and provide office space for its growing administration needs. This increased the popularity of the church, particularly with the younger generation, who were attracted partly to the high quality worship music, although there was also a natural follow through from the youth ministry.

Following this phase, the Vine acquired new premises in Wanchai. They took over what had been a movie theatre and refurbished the premises. Today the church continues to thrive with the new generation of leadership.

To me this is a good example of how common vision,

determination and hard work can achieve great things from humble beginnings. In my professional life, I always try to encourage students to clarify their vision and hopes, dreams and aspirations, because I know that often they underestimate themselves. An educator must inspire children to believe in themselves, and believe that they can make a difference in this troubled world. I feel we can do good with our time on earth, but our lack of belief often holds us back. I think having a good mentor can be an enormous help in preparation for each headship. Brian Driver had been that for me in the year when I worked with him at West Island School.

At that time it was right to spread my net beyond Hong Kong to look for the next career challenge. I was also motivated by the challenges of bringing up four teenage children in Hong Kong, as the city is extremely safe by western standards and it is very easy to get around.

My son Peter saw himself as a future skateboard star and would invest in different skate spots around Hong Kong. A lot of his friends had access to their parents' clubs and partied in top class hotels as well. He started to stay out later and later, and mealtimes together became a thing of the past. His grades at school began to plummet, and we were very concerned he was not developing the skills necessary for academic success. His life had got completely out of balance.

Interestingly, both Peter and Katy asked if we could please move from HK to have better friends. Katy's circle was experimenting with shoplifting at the time. It seemed to me that the only way to rescue this situation was to take them out of the environment of Hong Kong, which had become a playground. I made a few job applications and was offered the job of High School Principal at St John's International School in Waterloo, Belgium.

As I deliberated about taking the job in Belgium I was in two minds, as I found the Belgium tax rate a little intimidating. I had two dreams that confirmed that this was the correct thing to do. In the first, I was pulling a chain out of the water. At first the chain looked very ordinary, but as I continued to pull, it changed to gold. The message I got from this was that things might not look too exciting right now but if I took the job, great things would happen. In the second dream, I was flying some kind of simple flying ship, but I did not really know how to handle it. As I relaxed, the flight became exhilarating. The message I took from this was that even though I was entering the unfamiliar, ultimately the future would be positive and enjoyable.

Moving to Belgium was in some ways a revolution in our experience, as we had never lived in mainland Europe before, yet at the same time it had feelings of familiarity in terms of starting somewhere new. I wrote the following poem to try and express these feelings. The idea of 'revolution' brings to mind memories of driving around the Brussels ring road and going many kilometres out of our way to find the correct exit.

Revolution

In my car I listen to the engine vibrating,
The pulsing fan pushing out the warm air.
In my mind, thoughts revolve like butter in the churn,
New images are formed in peace and in pain,

Round and down and upwards, they come at me again,
Familiar yet strange, different but the same,
Now reincarnated but on a different plane.
Driving around the ring road circling Brussels,
A vortex is pulling me to the heart of the Grand Place,
Through the Sablon's slippery streets, Nirvana's gateway,
To what was once visited, now visited again,
For I have been around this square before,
Seen those fiery wheels within wheels,
And the old apocalyptic vision is reborn,
Slowly thickening, substantiating.
At a higher plane.
A new revolution beginning,
As I take the wheel again.

CHAPTER SIX

BELGIUM

Madeleine and James were both at college, so we made the move from Hong Kong to Belgium with just Katy and Peter. The transition for Peter was particularly tough. He missed the life in Hong Kong and they both felt bullied by some of the students at school, particularly as I was the new Principal, making changes that some students did not like. For example, the first day at school I went to the bakery next to the school, which students were allowed to visit. To my shock and horror, I saw about twenty students from the school smoking. This was clearly quite an established activity among the students.

It was also a tradition at the school that the seniors

would give 'wedgies' to the Year 9 students. This is where the Year 9 kids would have their trousers pulled up tight round their private parts, often causing considerable pain.

Looking more closely, there were no established rules or consequences and no established pastoral care system. Two of my early changes were to introduce rules and consequences and to set up a head of year system to enforce the rules and provide counselling. This obviously curtailed some of the activities that some of the students were used to indulging in. This did not make me popular with some of the students initially, but over time it created a respect for the school from within and also outside the school community. I also worked on raising academic standards through classroom visits and one-on-one appraisals with each teacher. Over time, our enrolment grew 25% and our IB average improved. Another area where we did well was in sport, where the school enjoyed a golden era. We were particularly successful at basketball, winning the International Schools Sports Tournament three consecutive years, with an 82-0 record of wins over the period.

Though Peter hated Belgium and went through a depressive stage, he did come closest to achieving his skateboard dream in Brussels. He sent his skateboard video to Globe, a leading skateboard company. They decided to sponsor him on the strength of this and he was furnished with new shoes, decks, hoodies and other clothing items.

Unfortunately his enthusiasm then began to wane. A factor in this may have been when he was practising his tricks in the school playground, and was singled out by a group of local boys. They surrounded him in an activity known as "steaming". He was in the centre of the circle with no way out except with the use of physical force. They stole his jacket, cash and skateboard. It took him quite a while to recover from this incident, which reinforced the fact that Europe was not as safe as HK. He found some consolation in joining the soccer team and, given his natural athletic talent, he was able to score a number of important goals. Peter eventually obtained his High School Graduation certificate and was offered a place at Leeds University to study Marketing. Kate got a place at Leeds Met to study Contemporary Creative Practice.

James had gone to Bangor University to study Criminology. He found that this was not for him and after a year back in Hong Kong working as a DJ, he went to SAE, a sound engineering school in London, and back in the digital world, he did extremely well. He was employed by a production company who made a number of programmes for the BBC. During this period he got to record a number of celebrities, including Ronnie Wood, Joss Stone, Amy Winehouse and many others.

Madeleine studied at Leeds University, which was the catalyst for the twins feeling confident to apply there. She went on to excel in teacher training at Trinity and All Saints College. She returned to Hong Kong to teach at King George V School, where she rapidly became Head of the Media Department.

James continued to excel in digital media production, perhaps as a natural outworking of his dyslexia, which gave him a unique advantage; it is interesting how sometimes our perceived weaknesses can somehow become our strengths and become more clearly defined over time. He went on to study at the National Film and Television School of the UK and gained work with leading post-production movie companies in Singapore and London. He worked on several major films, including *Hunger Games, Thor II* and *Fast and Furious 6.*

Besides the success at St. John's in academics, enrolments grew steadily, including members of the royal family of Belgium and Luxembourg. This was due not only to a more disciplined student body, improved academics and a highly successful sports programme, but just as important, to the building developments taking place. The High School was being refurbished, the labs, which had looked like something from Harry Potter, were completely remodelled and a new gym was built. A Performing Arts Centre was also added to the developing campus.

These developments definitely took our school to the next level. Unfortunately, from a timing perspective, there were challenges. 9/11 made American corporations more reserved in their employment of US nationals overseas. This hit enrolment, particularly in the Elementary School, which created financial strain for the school. I enjoyed being part of the European IB network at the time. Our school was well-known and highly respected at the IB conferences we attended. Alison and I had the opportunity to visit a number of European centres hosting these conferences, and we appreciated being able to visit Barcelona, Berlin, Hamburg, Stavanger, Sorrento, Prague, Dubrovnik and Budapest.

We enjoyed the vibrancy of Europe, which was more dynamic and culturally rich than we had expected. We enjoyed touring in France, Christmas fairs in Aachen and Monschau in Germany, cruising down the Rhine, walking the lanes of Venice and catching sight of Picasso and Monet's joint exhibition in Paris.

Though Belgian weather left something to be desired in terms of sunshine, its location was perfect for exploring Europe. During our first year in Belgium we decided to try skiing and snowboarding, as a request for chaperones for the high school trip was put out. We accompanied a school trip to St Johannes in Austria. I've never felt so cold in my life. I wish I could give a good report of my snowboarding experience, but the success was limited. I found that I could run down the beginners' slope quite quickly and with a certain amount of style. Unfortunately, stopping was another matter. I pulled my board sideways to attempt a stop, only for it to catch on some ice from the previous day's runoff.

Next thing I knew, I had fallen over backwards, cracking my head. I was not wearing a helmet and had knocked myself out on the ice. The Australian instructor decided to send me to hospital for a check-up after I kept repeating the question 'Why am I here?' They kept me in hospital for two days of observation. My roommate was a cheery older man who had a damaged shoulder from a ski accident. He said "Call me Fritz, I am from Austria." I asked him what he did for a living and he said that he was a ski instructor. Obviously, he had been having an off day. Every so often he would joke with me and say "Let's go down to the pub, Nick, let's have some schnapps". We neither of us were in any condition to go to the pub. When he realised I was British, he got a little bit defensive and said "I think they talk too much about the war".

Fortunately for me, nothing was broken. After a couple

of days, I was released from the hospital. As you might imagine, this curtailed my interest in snowboarding and from then on I took trips to Florida in the February breaks to see my lifelong friend Jym Kay. The weather in Florida suited us much better.

I did get to spend more time with the leader of that trip, Patrick, an Irishman, who spoke four European languages and had lived in Spain during the Franco era. Though that was the end of my snowboarding adventures, Patrick took the trip again the following year.

He was faced with a difficult disciplinary incident. A student got drunk on Jaegermeister during the overnight trip from Brussels to Austria and threw his mattress and all the bedding out of the train window. When he arrived in St Johannes, he went to the pub, where he took a lady's coat from the coat stand. He went through the pockets and found some Mercedes car keys, which he threw into the river. He then panicked and gave another student a lot of money to try to retrieve the keys, which could not be found. Patrick reported the situation to me when he got back to school. The student became one of the 21 students I asked to leave the school over this seven-year period I was Head.

Asking a student to leave is always one of the saddest jobs that a Head has to do. However, expelling a student sends a very clear message to the community that the school has a bottom line when it comes to the safety of everyone. I think it is essential that every student feels safe in school and taking strong action when appropriate is one way a head can reinforce that sense of security and safety. Other expulsions were triggered by such things as serious theft, which always intrigued me as all the students came from wealthy homes. Drugs were easily available from Holland.

My friend Patrick had his own share of mishaps. Even though he was an older man, he had never married. One day he surprised us all by announcing he was getting married to a Thai girl. The wedding duly took place, followed by a trip to Thailand, where he contracted hepatitis in its most deadly form. Fortunately he made a slow but steady recovery. He also became increasingly convinced that his contraction of hepatitis had not been accidental. He became certain that he had been deliberately infected so that his new wife would inherit all his wealth. His new mother-in-law was later held in a criminal investigation. That instituted divorce proceedings and the church was sympathetic to his cause, declaring the marriage null and void. It was a terrible physical and emotional trauma for Patrick to endure.

Whilst in Belgium, I was blessed with making two more close friends who were like brothers to me. The first of these was Terry, who was a pastor of our local church, an international style church which was always full on Sundays. I very much enjoyed playing guitar in their worship band and leading on a regular basis. I would meet Terry each Thursday in the bar of the Grand Hotel.

Over time, we got to know Nizah, the barman at the Grand Hotel. One day he surprised me by asking if he could borrow my car to go to a wedding.

Over the years I've been blessed with some wonderful cars, which I've enjoyed immensely. At that time I had a BMW 645. I realised I was taking a risk, but felt I wanted to share my good fortune with Nizah, so I took the chance and let him take the car. He returned it in perfect condition and I think he was touched by this simple act of trust. Certainly the standard of service that Terry and I enjoyed on our subsequent weekly trips improved significantly. An unexpected outcome.

Terry told me that if he had not been a pastor, he would have liked to have been either a policeman or a football coach. Helpfully he practised his coaching skills on me, and would advise on strategies during the week with ideas for handling each of the difficult situations I was facing. He was a great encourager and would remind me of the growth and success of the school year on year, citing academics, sports, arts facilities, growth in student numbers and the addition of a member of the Royal Family to the student body. He has remained a treasured friend up to the present time, and as part of his preaching schedule he recently visited us in Singapore.

Once when I said I was planning a trip to Venice with Alison, he jumped on that right away and said, "You can go alone if you want, but you know it would be much more fun with me". Terry had spent several years in Rome, leading an international church, and was well versed in Italian, so our next trip was to Rome, and it was certainly a lot more fun with Terry and his wonderful wife, Ruthanne.

We made a trip to the Trevi Fountain and pretty soon got distracted by the shoe shops nearby. Inevitably Alison and I left with a few pairs each of fine Italian style shoes. Alison's black sparkly trainers were thoroughly worn until they fell apart, but other more extreme designs have stayed in the closet, still beautiful, still unworn.

Terry was gloriously happy with a brand new pair of rubber-soled shoes. These were just what he wanted and needed. He wouldn't think of buying more as he was perfectly happy with this one new pair. It was rewarding to see someone so content and happy with a new pair of shoes.

Terry was originally from Texas, as was my second close friend in Belgium, Joe. He was the Director of my school. Joe was very proud of his Texan origin and he used to remind us regularly that Texas had special status, in that it had the right to cede from the Union. He had served with the US Marines in the Vietnam conflict but had moved into education on leaving the military. In Texas, he became a school supervisor before he left the US to take up a position in Europe.

Joe always impressed me with his combination of analytical skills, a focus on getting to know children personally, being visible and his tremendous integrity. He and his lovely wife Martha were strong Roman Catholics and they truly attempted to live out their faith in a way that influenced lives for good. They remain good friends to this day.

Joe's other main religion was sport. He was an avid supporter of the San Antonio Spurs, but his favourite sport was American football. St John's did not play American football, so he decided to take me for my induction to the International School at Brussels. I did not understand the grunts and other tribal sounds that the players emitted on a frequent basis. He tried hard to explain the mechanics of the game and the extremely technical rules. I think it was a bit like an Australian trying to explain cricket to an American. Of course, I remained convinced that rugby union was a superior game to American football with its accompanying body armour. Equally I'm sure an American would much prefer baseball, which I always thought of as a form of rounders, to cricket.

However, out of respect for Joe, on my next trip to the USA I did attend a game between the Milwaukee Brewers and the Atlanta Braves at Turner Field in Atlanta. The drama of the occasion was quite persuasive, and should I live in America I'm sure I would attend more games.

Terry was one of the finest pastors I have ever known. This is because he conveyed a genuine love for people. His messages were messages of encouragement. He communicated the idea that God loves people regardless of the shortcomings and failures we all have. This approach, which emphasised God's greatness, was very helpful to many people, and his church was always packed. He has about a million Facebook friends, which attests to his effectiveness in expressing God's love to needy people. His wife Ruthanne was second generation Italian and made the most outstanding tiramisu that you are ever likely to taste.

Belgium had given us a chance to see Europe, which I found surprisingly dynamic and exceeded my expectations in many ways. Courtesy of the Channel Tunnel between UK and France, it also gave me the chance to visit my mother in Warwickshire several times a year. It was about six hours door to door. My V8-powered BMW carried Belgian plates, which I had soon discovered meant that I did not get speeding tickets in the UK. Our finance manager was not so lucky when he went down to France; he was cruising at about 180km/hr in his truck in pouring rain. He passed a speed camera, and then a few minutes later he was pulled over by the French police. They took him to a police station in a small rural area, confiscated his licence and compounded his vehicle, plus he had to pay an enormous fine. His bigger problem however, was how would he get home? There was no railway station and no bus service. Walking back to Belgium did not seem a viable option, partly because he had been a professional basketball player out of Dukes University and now his ankles and knees were shot. Sadly, a while later he had an operation to fix artificial ankles, which went wrong, and he passed away at the age of 59 which was a sad loss. Strange thing was that he passed away after I had left the school and I had a dream in which he was calling out to me and basically saying 'goodbye'.

As to how he got back from France, he called his wife in Belgium, who hired a taxi to drive down and bring him up. I should think it cost most of his month's salary. My take-away from that story was not to speed in France, tempting as the roads were.

Speaking of music, church and inspiration, in Belgium I continued to enjoy playing in the church worship band; however, I began to find some of the songs rather trite. As a writer of Christian music, I wanted to feel a deeper connection with the material. I feel that our relationship with God should be a romance: he enchants us with the beauty of nature, the seasons, the light, the stars and particularly with the wonder of relationships with those closest to us. So I came up with a plan. First I wanted to explore the romance through original poetry and songs, culminating in the production of a CD. My plan for this was to use the momentum from the first romance CD, which I called 'The Pilgrim of Love' to create a new worship CD where the focus was on the romance of our relationship with

Jesus. These are the lyrics of two of the songs:

Queen of romance

Like a dreaming angel in silver and white
Mystic fairy princess you rule the night
Here in the castle, a soft candle glow
As you work your magic, bind my heart to your own
Enchanted I watched you dance
I am enraptured by the Queen of Romance
Many voices echo, but I hear only yours
Wind within my sails whispering my course
The mystery of love is like a magic tune
I am following your fragrant Arabian perfume
Romance is a mystery
Romance is a dream
Romance is a question
You are my answer babe I believe
Now I see you beckon, offering your hand
Coachman, horses await your command
secret delights, pleasures you've planned
I don't know how I got here but before you I stand
Transported I witnessed you move
my heart's been captured by a queen I dreamed I knew.

Affinity

The sun shares its diamonds with the morning dew
The night time brings silence as I dream of you
Cool the rain brings refreshment to the forest trees
And the dawn gives me hope of what is yet to be

Affinity, affinity, moon and the sea
That's you and me
Affinity for eternity, forever and free,
That's you and me
The morning brings sparkles to the eyes of the sea
And the rainbow is searching for the place you might be
The mist shares its secrets with the mountain breeze
And the sunset brings me visions of a love that's free
Hey darling, I know our love will never ever fade away
Because your love sustains my love
And love's an eternal flame
The river rushes to embrace the sea
And time gives its moments to eternity
And the sun is shining to reveal your beauty
And love shares its blindness so i can see
Affinity, affinity
The moon and the sea
That's you and me
Affinity for eternity
Forever and free
That's you and me
Affinity for eternity
Together and free
That's you and me
The sunset, the sunset was made for you and me
The sunset, the sunset burns for you and me
Together and free
That's just how it's gonna be
For eternity.

I used a producer for the album *Pilgrim of Love* who was

able to arrange the songs and add some dynamic instrumentation. All the brass was played live, and so were the strings. We had some wonderful black backing singers who did a great job supporting my vocals. In terms of production quality this was the best record I had produced up to that point. However, the downside for me was that some of the grooves were not as I had imagined them to be. We recorded the album at the Kaiser Chiefs' studio in Leeds, England. The cover photography was done by my long-term friend David Mackintyre.

David had been a freelance photographer. The most daring assignment he undertook was going to meet with Abu Sayyaf, a radical Islamist group based in the southern Philippines who had kidnapped several German tourists. His pictures were published in *Stern* magazine in Germany. He was lucky not to be taken captive by the group. They let him go in order to publicize the pictures, which caused fear. The only thing he lost was his watch, which one of the terrorists took a liking to. He also did the cover picture for my earlier album, *Stranger*.

The arts support group at St Johns asked me if I could think of a new event that could be put on at the school to give the arts wider exposure. I suggested that I could bring over the producer, guitarist and choir director who had worked on the album to work with the students to put on a concert, and at the same time I would play songs from my new record. The parents loved the idea and we put the plan into action. The various experts worked with the choir and bands to enable them to reach a standard of excellence in the song they wanted to play at the concert. At the end of the week, we brought in a big professional PA system and we were set to go. The theatre was crowded out and the event was a huge success. We called the event 'The School of Rock' because of the similarity to the movie of the same name.

Our school had become well regarded, and High School enrolment had risen considerably. The challenge of school improvement was being met, school culture was strong and results were excellent. I began to look for other school leadership opportunities and challenges. Offers I received included posts in Brunei and Dallas and led ultimately to the new school opportunity in Hong Kong.

Much as I had enjoyed my time in Belgium, the mood in the school was beginning to change. This coincided with a skype call from Hong Kong; one of my long-term friends was asking me to return. He was the chairman of the YMCA and had previously been an elder in the Vine Church. The YMCA had acquired a secondary school. However, things were not going well in terms of the relationship between the Board and the Principal. The Board wanted to terminate the Principal's employment with the school. Consequently they had a meeting of parents, with the Board, to discuss the issues. The Principal had arranged her supporters very well. She was a very experienced and intelligent lady, but very much in the traditional mode, and she had run the school in a very autocratic way. There were those who supported this traditional approach, especially as she had previously been head of a prestigious school. There were also those who found her unapproachable and impossible to have a dialogue with.

At the meeting between the Board and the parents, the supporters were very vocal in their support of the Principal. Two issues that had surfaced in public had made the Board members feel extremely embarrassed, and the Chairman in his Skype call said he didn't want to deal with the situation any more. He had been badly offended and felt that his authority had been undermined in public. He and his colleagues felt so strongly that he was considering selling the school. There was another option: he said he thought I could fix this situation, and asked me to return to Hong Kong.

CHAPTER SEVEN

RETURN TO HONG KONG

I told the Chairman that in order to effect change, I needed a position senior to the Principal in the Hong Kong school. In law, each school in HK has a supervisor who holds ultimate responsibility for school operations. It was agreed that I would become the School Supervisor.

So over the next few days we negotiated a salary and a start date. As I was Supervisor of the school, the Principal had to run all decisions past me. She had managed to negotiate an extra year running the school. My approach was to work with her and offer her as much support as possible. This coincided with the school's government education department inspection. She wanted the school to look as good as possible and she thought that I could help her with preparations for the inspection, which I did.

The school was in the particular category of Direct Subsidy Schools. This meant it had some flexibility with the curriculum and could also charge fees. Even though the majority of the teachers were Chinese, the medium of instruction was supposed to be English. I soon discovered that if the class did not have any Westerners, then the default mode was to teach the lessons in Cantonese. I was also shocked to see students sleeping with their heads on the desk completely unchallenged by the teacher.

I had joined the school in December, which gave me six months to make observations and plans for things that I wanted to do with the school when the current Principal left in the summer. I also took into my confidence a sort of shadow cabinet who would become my leaders in due course so that we could advance plans ready for the following September.

I think it's very important for a school to have a point of difference. YHKCC had just 30% non-local students, while the other 70% were local Chinese. I was aware that many expat families could not afford the fees from the major international schools. Our school had a special status that allowed us to charge lower fees and also to receive government subsidies, if we adhered to the Education Department guidelines. Fortunately these guidelines gave us a lot of latitude with the curriculum, so very early on in my tenure I took the opportunity to introduce IGCsE for the 14-16 year olds; this was the most internationally-favoured examination for this age group.

For 17-18 year olds, I introduced British A levels, as I noticed that every school in HK seemed to have migrated to the IB diploma. The IB diploma is a great education and a very good platform, but certainly not for all children as it demands that children study five subjects, while volunteering, community service, an extended essay and 'theory of knowledge' are compulsory in addition. Therefore for some students A levels are an easier route to university, as students can choose subjects that suit them and cover fewer subjects.

These two examination pathways created our "point of difference" in the Hong Kong education market, giving an option for families to benefit from an international education at an affordable price.

I also cracked down on teachers who were teaching in Cantonese and warned teachers that they would not be allowed to use microphones in the classroom, as I felt this led to a lecture style of teaching rather than the interactive style I wanted.

We were blessed with a sports field, which is very rare in HK because of space restrictions.

Within three years we had increased enrolment by 30% and for each year the ratio of Chinese to Western students had changed until there were now about 70% non-Chinese students. The gap in the market that we had identified was drawing in a wide range of nationalities, about 50 in total. Parental confidence grew rapidly and along with this our waiting lists grew. Our leadership team was a wonderful blend of Chinese and Western leaders.

There was no friction between the races, and the team was very engaged and positive. As a result this leadership team was aware that we were building something original and successful. This was a very joyful, positive experience. We were building a programme which resulted in state-of-the-art music facilities and extra spaces. These improvements were funded by the surplus that the school generated.

Despite the success we experienced in Hong Kong at YHKCC, I did not feel well treated by some board members and, looking at my age, I decided to move one last time. I had always loved small children, but I had never run a school that covered the whole age range. I wanted this challenge before I concluded my career.

CHAPTER EIGHT

THE FINAL ROUND: SINGAPORE AND HOME

I applied for principal leadership positions to a number of all-through schools and was offered opportunities in Dubai, Bangkok and Singapore. The Singapore option of the Australian International School (AIS) seemed most attractive to me because of the size of the school; it was bigger than any other (2,600 pupils) and I could see that there were plenty of opportunities to improve it. The school was a for-profit school, which was a first for me. I rationalized it by thinking that all schools need to turn a profit to enable development of its facilities.

I asked the owners if I could have a six-week overlap period with the outgoing head so that I could get to understand the school culture and also investigate the feelings of the parents and the students about the school. The research was quite shocking. I began by looking at the exit interview data from parents who had chosen to leave the school. I then looked at the statistics of parents who withdrew their children. This was focused most intensely around the middle years, with over a hundred students leaving per year. The main reason parents gave for withdrawing their children was poor academic standards; they also felt that they did not have a voice in the school and that complaints were largely ignored. I also held some "town hall" meetings where I asked parents to express their feelings and also to describe to me how they would describe Australian culture, since about 70% of the school was made up of Australians.

The other main complaint was the weakness of the sports programme. I had expected the school to have a flourishing sports programme, given the fact that Australian culture values sport very highly. In fact, the sports programme was virtually non-existent. The main reason for this was that the school ran on the Southern Hemisphere calendar school year, whereas other international schools were run on the Northern Hemisphere school calendar. This therefore created difficulties in arranging sports fixtures. This excuse was very disappointing to me, as I believe that where there is real determination most problems can be solved.

My arrival coincided with the arrival of the new head of sports, Justin Teves. We immediately struck up a very strong bond and vision for how we could develop the sports programme. Our plan included starting a league of Australian schools in the region. This would be an opportunity to have sporting exchanges with other schools operating on the same calendar and create valuable competition experience for our athletes.

I was keen to see the creation of a swimming club run by school coaches which up to then had been outsourced. Given the powerful role of sports in young people's lives, I told Justin that as we got going on sports, we would become like an unstoppable freight train, which is exactly what happened. Today, we probably have the most elite sports programme in Singapore.

All the developments that I envisaged I documented in the form of a school development plan so that everybody could see the track we were on. The plan was specific and time related. I am a big believer in the creation of plans and accountability within those plans, so each term I would get staff who were responsible for various elements of the plan to report back to the whole staff. This helped to generate a sense of momentum and clear direction for the school. I included parents in the feedback on our development plan.

The next thing I did was to develop a new vision and values statement. I used an outside facilitator to get us started on the process. She did a fantastic job, and the project was then put in the hands of a working group of about eight people to finalize the actual statements themselves, drawing on input from parents, staff and students.

The three core words that we came up with were **respect**, which was the core of how we wanted relationships to work in the school; **achievement**, because at the end of the day the school must enable students to achieve their potential academically so they can access the most creative and fulfilling of the careers available to them, and finally, **opportunity**. I think it is the responsibility of any school to provide as many opportunities as possible for students to discover and develop their talents. Things that start as hobbies can sometimes become careers, or at least provide a platform for lifelong enjoyment.

Because all the staff had been involved in the process of creating new guiding statements, there was a high level of acceptance of the new direction that the statements provided. At the same time, we changed the logo of the school. This was facilitated by one of the design experts Landor, who undertook the work pro bono. The new design was strong and modern, and there was opportunity for modification according to how it was applied.

The final piece in the change of direction was the introduction of the new school uniform. The school up to that point had five different uniforms, all slightly different shades of green. It looked as if it might have been designed by Steve Irwin, the late TV wildlife presenter. This was one of the toughest and most controversial changes. There was even a Facebook page started by opponents of the change. However, we battled through and now people frequently tell me that they have the most elegant uniform in Singapore.

Other problems we faced were the absence of a systematic mapping of the curriculum, which meant that there were no standards that the curriculum was linked to. There was some testing, but this wasn't looked at systematically and there were no examinations of year-on-year data to show student growth. Also there was a lack of examination practice, with the first exams being in year 10.

The way teachers were recruited was another problem.

All recruitment was handled by two people who had only a loose idea of what the staffing needs might be. This meant that teachers who were newly recruited might find themselves teaching age groups or subjects that they were not experienced in. Also there is no way that two people can have the appropriate expertise to recruit the best candidates from pre-school to Year 12. So we involved heads of school, and the recruitment process was done mostly by Skype, except for senior positions. I appointed two staff, one for elementary and one for secondary, to analyse data and make recommendations on how we could improve teaching and achieve better results and track year by year, particularly in relation to Australia's highest performing territory, which is ASCT, Australia's capital territory. The use of data was generally overseen by heads of departments; previously they had been responsible only for years 10, 11 and 12. I extended this to cover the curriculum from years 6-12 and secondary.

Another problem we had was that the school had been divided up into five self-managing sub-schools. The teachers complained that communication between the sub-schools was poor, particularly in relation to curriculum continuity and progression. As a result I did away with the middle school and created one secondary school. The middle school was where we were losing most students to other international schools due to poor academic standards. For example, in Science they would spend a whole term looking at the properties of popcorn. Their introduction to the Middle Years Programme was to decorate a cookie. Not all teachers were sold on the MYP and were not using the assessment criteria, so the application of the programme was very uneven.

In Elementary I joined the preschool, lower and upper schools together and rearranged the structure with a Head of Elementary and oversight of curriculum, continuity and progression, and a Head of Curriculum and a Head of Welfare for each year. In secondary I appointed a Head of School after a period of time of handling this myself. In addition to the Head of School role, we appointed two pastoral heads of year per year group, and created school rules and consequences. The idea of school rules and consequences may be obvious, but I was told by staff that their preventative programmes and quality of relationships with the students had taken them beyond the need for rules.

One of the main proponents of this point of view came to see me one day. She had a problem. A student had taken a picture of a girl topless at a party and had shared the picture, so I asked her what the preventative measures were. She said that there had been a lecture on this kind of behaviour the previous week. Obviously in this case, it had failed to achieve its objective. I asked her what she intended to do about this, as the Head of Welfare and she said, "I think I need to suspend this student". I said, "I think you are right". The point was made and within a short time a new behaviour policy was in place.

So the use of data, the restructuring of the schools and the introduction of new policies all worked together to give us a much more rigorous environment. By using data, we could see how in some areas students had actually regressed in their learning. We could see that we had put a stop to this and parent confidence improved so that the flood of relocations to other schools became a dribble with some students actually returning from boarding schools. This all took place during the first year of my tenure, and there was a lot of opposition from staff. Some of the opposition was tied to the fact that I was British, even though I hadn't lived in the UK for 30 years. I had been warned that Australians hate change and have a very strong sense of mateship, which meant that there were coalitions opposing the change; certainly, it was unfashionable to show or offer support for the changes initially.

I remember standing up in a Secondary staff meeting and saying that if people didn't like the changes, they had an option, as I did. I said the school was a like a ship; this was the direction we were going in with the support of the board and the owners. After the end of the first year, a number of Middle School dissenters chose to move on because the impact of the proposed changes would affect them the most. At the next recruitment a number of new staff joined the school, excited at the prospect of being part of a school going through such transformations. They brought with them a sense of enthusiasm and commitment to the change agenda. Many of them were already familiar with the measures being introduced to bring about positive change. From then on, things improved tremendously. The openness to change was very motivating and we completed our four-year development plan within two years.

To create change it is necessary to have a team of people who believe in what you are doing and trying to create. The big challenge with AIS was that there were very few people who had experience of working in a top international school. Most teachers had limited experience, and this came mostly from working in state schools in Australia, so the possibility of building a base of staff who would understand the direction and vision for the future was very limited. The core value of mateship also provided an obstacle, because to cooperate with the new head was in some sense a betrayal of that value in the school. The team of deputies in particular had a strong alliance which was wedded to their understanding of the IB philosophy. When they were asked to implement initiatives that did not coincide with their views, they chose not to implement them, or actively opposed them. Opposition included forming groups of parents who were encouraged to also voice opposition to particular change. Often these groups were actually furnished with questions that they should ask me in order to oppose the changes. This was particularly the case with the change from MYP to IGCSE, even though the weak curriculum in this area was the number one negative concern of the majority of parents.

The other area where we experienced organised opposition was in the area of uniform change. A Facebook page was set up to fight the new uniform. One item of the uniform I was prepared to negotiate on was the boys' shirts. The Facebook group wanted a white shirt for the younger students instead of the blue striped shirt that we were proposing. Since they felt strongly about this, I would put it to a parent vote. I was shocked to discover that the group was spreading a method to cheat on the parent vote, so that they could vote multiple times. At this point the matter had become ridiculous and I withdrew the opportunity to vote. This turned out to be a good decision, as many parents contacted me to express their disgust with the actions of the group and fully supported the school's action on the matter. My main supporters came from the head of marketing,

Katrina Bracken, who withstood her own barrage of opposition, and the head of the parents' association, Tara Milne, who not only understood the needs and wishes of the parents but was deeply committed to action that would support the new vision.

I was eventually able to recruit a new Head of Secondary who was an Australian but with international experience of some very good schools. He knew the kind of level I was aspiring to and his support was deeply valued. I also hired an administrator who was Australian but had experience at the Harris Academy in the UK, which had an outstanding reputation for turning schools around, particularly through the use of data.

My metaphor for leading change is that you can progress faster if you have the right team of horses pulling your chariot. Slowly but surely we were getting that team together. I also felt it was important to have some objective measure of the development of the school. I therefore contacted the ex-Chief Inspector of Schools for Scotland, Archie McGlen, and the ex-Primary Education Officer for the English Schools Foundation in Hong Kong, David Coles, to act as 'critical friends' in a long-term review process. I asked them to do a review of the school and publish a report. Their first report was quite damning and was strongly opposed by the provisional group of deputies. I think they thought I'd had a hand in writing it. However I am pleased to say that their follow-up reports in subsequent years were increasingly positive and their final report judged the school as excellent. Looking at it from an Ofsted perspective, this was a huge affirmation of the transformation of the school over time.

Such long-term critical friend reviews could I believe be a significant help in school improvement. Reviewers can get to know the school in considerable detail and track both the strengths and weaknesses of school over time and offer advice on improvement. Comments were gathered from a group of staff, parents and students reflecting on the observable evidence of the transformations of 2012-2014.

2012 had been a very tough year but immensely successful, as we set a new standard and direction for AIS. In May my mother passed away and I went to the UK to share in her funeral service. We tried to follow her wishes for the funeral as she had already prepared instructions for us, which included my playing two of my own songs which she had enjoyed. These were *I Can See Angels* from the musical *Carpenter King* and *Eagle's Wings,* which is on my *Stranger* album. The words for this are as follows:

Eagles' wings

When troubles come

When sorrows fall

When streams have all run dry and no-one seems to care at all

Rise up on eagle's wings,

You can go higher and higher.

Lost ones are loved and loved ones are lost

Temptation to lose faith

Don't even stop to count the cost

I can almost touch the sun

Light shining on everyone

In the spirit I can fly away

Spirit trapped inside
Take your wings away and fly far far above, above this world
To where the angels glide

As I was playing this song I noticed a trembling in my left leg. I didn't think much about it at the time. In June I was invited to speak at the Young President's Organisation conference in Chiang Mai. During some downtime, as Alison and I took some bikes and rode around the Four Seasons resort, I noticed that my balance was not good and I actually fell. I have always been athletic and maintained a healthy regime, so I found this quite inexplicable.

When we got back to Singapore I booked in with a physiotherapist, who gave me various exercises to do to strengthen my leg. I didn't feel these were getting to the root of the problem. I then went to a chiropractor, who also was unable to help. Finally a doctor suggested that I visit Kings College Hospital in London. I was able to do this in November, as there was a Cognita conference to recognise the best teachers from Cognita schools across the world.

When I saw the neurologist Cathy Ellis, she gave me the diagnosis. I had contracted the degenerative disease ALS, a form of motor neurone disease.

It is often said in speeches 'what would you do, or change, if it was the last day of your life?' I've always tried to live in such a way that if today was the last day, I would be completely satisfied. I was fortunate to become a teacher, although it was not what I set out to be. Actually, it was my wife's suggestion. My preference would have been to do music. However, this is a difficult field in which to make a consistent living, and by the time our first child Madeleine had been born, I knew I needed a steady job.

I found the teaching practices invigorating and enjoyable. Teaching involves a blend of imparting knowledge or helping kids to gain understanding to prepare them for a better future and to keep their interest through stimulating resources and a bit of play-acting. Looking back, I can think of no more meaningful way to use your life than in giving young people belief in themselves so that they can achieve their dreams, become significant people in their own right and make a difference for good in this needy world.

For me, teaching has been a great vocation, something I was meant to do. So when I received the diagnosis, there was no question for me about giving up work. I wanted to remain engaged with the students for as long as I could. I continued to visit classrooms as best I could, and attended sports events. I also continued with my one-to-one meetings with key leadership staff in the school. By mid-2014, the owners had decided that it was prudent to put in an acting principal and my Head of Secondary, Andre Casson, was promoted to this position.

I found leaving the school difficult, as this was the crown of my professional work and I missed the students a great deal. However, a number of key staff continued to visit me at my home to give me updates and seek my advice. A student I had been mentoring, Jordy Gray, also continued to visit me. I had encouraged her passion for Formula One, and at this time it looks as if she will be offered an internship with Ferrari. She got me two Ferrari hats, one signed by Niki Lauda with the message "Stay strong", and the other signed by Fernando Alonzo and a former student of mine, Jerome Ambrosio, who was the reserve driver for Lotus.

I regard each day as a gift and a chance to know God better and to encourage others. I have been overwhelmed by messages and visits from old friends, ex-students and colleagues. Each day is rich and valuable; life should be lived in the moment. Life is often wasted in regretting the past or feeling what the future might be. We should be absorbed in the things that we have true passion for. I think schools should help students to discover those passions through providing wonderful broad opportunities for them to try new experiences.

I am also a big supporter of pastoral care for students to enable them to achieve their potential. They need to feel safe and cared about. For me, the best teachers are those are who not only convey a passion for learning but a sense of love for their students. Within these parameters, students learn best. Also, I believe that a very clear discipline policy is essential in creating that sense of safety and security. Finally, we cannot dodge the question of achievement. In this regard, testing is useful, taken in conjunction with an understanding of the learning needs of each child. It is important that the school's philosophy and beliefs are clearly articulated and lived out in all interchanges with staff, students and parents.

I believe a school is first and foremost a culture and that culture is formed by a strong community. People need to know what the community stands for, and this needs to be clearly articulated on a regular basis by the school's leadership. To get a clear idea of how effective the school is, all forms of evaluation are useful. These must include a combination of internal evaluations and constant monitoring by senior and middle managers and external verification against clear standards. These findings will inform teacher improvement, as expressed in the school improvement plan. If the school is not moving forward it will certainly regress. Complex though schools are, we must never forget that they exist for the sake of the students. We are there to give the students the best possible future.

Stranger

When the darkness crowds about me,
I can see that I've been so blind
And my eyes weep silver tears
To wash away the darkness that I find
People seem to stop and stare,
Makes me wish that I was not there
But the dance it soothes my eyes
Someone telling me that they care.

Chorus:
I'm just a stranger in this world
Just passing through
Got a home on high
That's where I'm sailing to, sailing to.

Tomorrow's a brand new day,
You can rise up high
If your sails are full of love
You can kiss the sky
And if you're sailing with Jesus
You'll never die
For the truth can't lie.

From Keith Peterson, Head of Arndell Junior School, New South Wales

Dear Alison

Thank you for your great kindness in telling me of Nick's death this morning.

The thing that I know best about Nick Miller is his passion for life; this great giftedness for life and for love that was a discipleship to the Lord Jesus as natural as breathing but as unboundedly 'cosmic' as the farthest, most beautiful star!

Nick once said to me, 'People think that to be a Christian is to be stuck into a mould so that you can never be yourself again. It's not. God's love sets us free to be truly ourselves. That's what love does. Sets us free to be our truest selves.'

I will never know anyone as full of life as Nick – or a Son so 'full of Jesus as the sky is full of stars'.

The vision for Jesus and the Kingdom that Nick imparted to me changed my life.

As Nick now is in the fullness of life, it's really my passionate hope that for the following season of my life – and particularly my life in education – I might find the grace to take something of the baton that he ran with such talent, insight, humanity, humble authority and grace - and run a little with it too...

So that in the days ahead – in school and university, church and family - whenever and wherever love wins – wherever love sings – I'll hear and celebrate too the song of Nick's legacy and touch again that eternal rhythm of the stars and of his totally generous friendship that for me turned ashes into beauty and hopelessness into the embrace of the running Father.

Oh Lord did I tell you you're like the most beautiful poem
I see your face in the stars tonight
Did the sun rise specially for you
Then flee, jealous of your light

It's gonna be alright
You'll see us through this night
In your love Lord Jesus
It's gonna be alright
It's gonna be alright
It's gonna be alright
– Nick Miller.

Much love to you Alison.
God bless
Keith